"Greg and Kent invite you on a journey ... ...nd
philosophy of Competency-Based The ...i-
tioners, explorers, and shepherds who .... path and
history of commitment to continuous improvement in offering student-driven,
mentor-supported, and human-centered technologically based contextual education. They don't shy away from big issues of affordability, accessibility, and
educational quality. Readers will be invited to rethink everything from mission
to assessment to governance in a quest to reconnect the academy and the church.
It's been a fascinating journey to track, and I trust what they offer will 'fan the
flame' and invite further exploration."

—Amy L. Kardash,
President,
In Trust Center for Theological Schools

"These two pioneers of Competency-Based Theological Education have done
the community of theological educators an outstanding service by gathering
and sharing their insights with us. Through their extensive experience they have
counseled numerous schools, tested innovative ideas and processes, and not
least of all provided learning for their colleagues on the ATS staff. Through this
volume, they are sharing their ever-growing expertise with a broader audience.
While some schools might not be willing nor able to implement full programs of
CBTE, most can benefit from some or all the ideas presented here. Perhaps most
importantly, Kent and Greg help us to identify and wrestle with fundamental
questions about the goals of theological education, the ways it is provided, and
what might be some contours of its future shape."

—Stephen Graham,
Strategic Director of Context and Continuity,
Director of Accrediting, Association of Theological Schools

"CBTE is disrupting (in a good way) our long-standing approach to theological education. It's not a 'fad' or a 'flash-in-the-pan' phenomenon. Rather, it's a
philosophy of education that is fundamentally changing theological education.
Anderson and Henson do a tremendous job of articulating how CBTE reimag-
ines the academy by centering on the triad—the church, the student, and the
institution. CBTE is producing the next generation of capable and well-equipped
ministry leaders. Interested in seeing how you can use CBTE at your institution?
This book will most certainly get you headed in the right direction."

—Philip Dearborn,
President,
Association for Biblical Higher Education

"Education should be designed around the learner—not the institution, curriculum, IT requirements, or business model. In an age where educational institutions and ed tech alike have grown bloated with administrative complexity, disconnection, and unsustainable costs, it's no surprise that students are increasingly opting out of traditional degree programs. This concise read provides a human-centered blueprint for redesigning every aspect of theological education around the learner and their mission within the church. It's an indispensable book for church leaders and educators looking to design a better path for theological education."

—Paul Johnson,
CEO and Cofounder,
Pathwright

"Kent and Greg were among the original pioneers of the CBTE movement in North America, and both have generously shared their insights and experiences with other theological educators for the past ten years. The story, philosophy, and resultant practices behind CBTE have been outlined through countless presentations and white papers, but in this book they are finally available as a thoughtfully articulated whole. Greg and Kent have done an excellent job of capturing the heart and core elements of CBTE, challenging us to refocus our telos on the ends of theological education and accept necessary disruption to the conventional means."

—Ruth McGillivray,
Executive Vice President,
Northwest Seminary and College

"The fundamental mission of CBTE is one every educator across disciplines can benefit from understanding: each learner must leave our learning experiences with more than skills. This book outlines how CBTE lends itself to not only measuring one's grasp of content and enduring understandings, but ensuring learners possess the character traits and dispositions that make us uniquely human: compassion, empathy, kindness, humility. These are the dispositions and competencies that take us beyond the skills of today and move us toward a better society."

—Lisa McIntyre-Hite,
Executive Vice President and Chief Operating Officer,
Competency-Based Education Network Solutions

"Greg and Kent have done a masterful job of identifying the key problem of seminaries—the disconnect between the academy and the church. What is the reason for the existence of the seminaries if not to develop leaders for the church to help fulfill the Great Commission motivated by his Great Commandment? Unless change takes place, seminaries run the risk of becoming irrelevant to the church. The educational philosophy of Competency-Based Theological Education is seen to help restore the relationship between the academy and the church, especially by focusing on the outcomes for the students. This book provokes us to consider new ways of coming together to develop leaders to be more effective for Christ in their context. This is a must-read as we adjust for the present and prepare for the future."

Henry Tan,
President,
International Leadership Consortium

"If you serve as a board member or administrator at a seminary or theological school, Anderson and Henson have done you a huge favor. Read this book to locate thoughtful insights and practical design ideas for restoring relevance and accessibility to the seminary experience, for renewing the relationship between the academy and the local church, and for renovating programs in the face of inevitable change. After reading it, you may continue to invite students to campus, but you will also discover ways to deliver seminary to students in every context."

—Gary G. Hoag,
President & CEO,
Global Trust Partners

"Competency-based models of education are not new, but they are new to theological education. In the moment when theological education urgently needs to be reimagined and recast, this text is right on time. Anderson and Henson, from their own ingenuity and experience, provide a detailed map for any seminary or divinity school interested in adapting this praxis-based approach. This book gives us the opportunity to learn from two of the foremost pedagogical engineers of our time. Replete with principles, practices, and design proposals, this book allows for in-depth consideration of this educational model. This book will make an excellent tool for any faculty developing or improving a competency-based curriculum."

—Nancy Lynne Westfield,
Director,
Wabash Center for Teaching and Learning in Theology and Religion

"Anderson and Henson have delivered a masterpiece for pastoral and church worker development. As a long-time faculty mentor engaged in a CBTE program, I can speak firsthand to how contextual, adaptable, affordable, and theologically rigorous CBTE is. It is my prayer that CBTE could deepen trust and collaboration between institutions and local churches in the much-needed task of leadership formation."

—Tim Ahlman,
Pastor,
Christ's Greenfield Lutheran Church and School

"Anderson and Henson provide an invaluable roadmap to an important educational paradigm shift. Their guide is grounded in the missional call to rediscover the heartbeat of theological education—namely, equipping disciple-making leaders for the church. *Theological Education* introduces readers to the contours of Competency-Based Theological Education (CBTE) and provides a pioneer's guide to effectively navigating uncharted terrain. There is much to learn from their collective experience and particular expressions of CBTE."

—Gabe Tribbett,
Director of Deploy (CBTE),
Grace Theological College and Seminary

"Greg's and Kent's expertise shines brightly in this groundbreaking work. Their book is a valuable resource for educators in the evolving landscape of competency-based education. It offers essential principles, practices, and practical suggestions for learning design. Their emphasis on formation, context, and community is especially timely and needed in this field. I'm grateful for the wisdom they've shared, and this book is a must-read for anyone looking to understand and implement competency-based education effectively."

—Charla Long,
President,
Competency-Based Education Network

THEOLOGICAL EDUCATION

Principles and Practices of a Competency-Based Approach

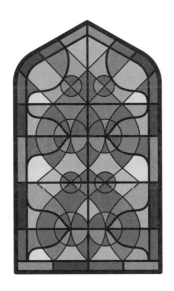

Kenton C. Anderson and
Gregory J. Henson

To our spouses, Karen and Heather,
who have not only walked with us but whose wisdom
is woven throughout these pages.

To those brave leaders in theological education who have
inspired us and opened doors for our creativity:
Daniel Aleshire, Charla Long, Leland Eliason, Tom Tanner,
Stephen Graham, David Williams, and Chris Meinzer,
along with a multitude of sojourners.

We are grateful for all of the people above,
trusting that this work might help to sustain their passion
for theological education and make the most of their
invitation to innovation as we follow Jesus.

CONTENTS

FOREWORD

By Tom Tanner

I'm delighted to write a foreword for this book by two of the most caring and innovative seminary leaders I have known: Greg Henson and Kent Anderson. When I first met them nearly ten years ago, their respective seminaries were—to be blunt—seriously struggling for survival. Northwest Seminary, which Kent then led, had been told by their denomination that unless things changed soon in how they prepared pastors for their churches there would not be a denomination left for them to serve. Sioux Falls Seminary, now Kairos University that Greg leads, was losing students and support so fast back then that their accreditors placed them on probation, giving them only two years to turn it around "or else."

That was then. A decade later their seminaries are thriving. Collectively, they now enroll more than a thousand students from across North America and dozens of countries worldwide. They have partnered with many other seminaries and mission agencies around the globe in ways that help all of them achieve their missions. Financially, they are doing well and getting stronger every year. They are recognized as "turn-around" seminaries within ATS. Their story is something of "a tale of two cities"—the *worst* of times that became the *best* of times. Their story, to be sure, is not every seminary's story, nor are their solutions the only solutions for every struggling seminary. But their story requires us to at least ask, "How did they do it?" This book tells not only *how* they did it, but *why* they did it. Their "why" is what commends this book to any theological educator or church leader who wants their institution to achieve their mission more faithfully and effectively.

This book, however, is not about their individual or institutional stories but about the story of CBTE, Competency-Based Theological Education. That term didn't exist a decade ago but has now become a global phenomenon with an annual conference that has drawn hundreds of participants from around the world since it began five years ago. In this book the two authors note that they "have worked with people from nearly one hundred countries, spread across six different continents, who speak an array of languages" (p. 99). While CBTE is often considered just another model or methodology, these two theological educators make the case that CBTE is much more than that, as Chapter Two on CBTE principles makes clear. One of the most telling and compelling statements is this one: "CBTE is not about delivering something; it is about walking with someone. It will allow mentors, learners, faculty, and administrators to develop learning pathways that meet people where they are and help them get to where they need to be in light of their call, context, and community" (pp. 80–81).

So, I invite you to set aside whatever doubts or disbeliefs you may have about CBTE as just another "quick fix" and journey instead with these two seminary leaders as they tell their story, not about their two seminaries, but about a new way of thinking about theological education. I invite you to read and to wrestle, as they have, with the things that matter most to our diverse missions. You will find here a story of humility and honesty, told with both passion and compassion. You might even find that their story is your story.

Tom Tanner served as director of accreditation for the ATS Commission on Accrediting for ten years (2012–2022). He was accreditation liaison to both Kent's and Greg's schools, helping Northwest Seminary receive the first-ever accreditation approval for a CBTE program and helping Kairos University expand its accreditation to partner with three other ATS seminaries through CBTE programs.

PREFACE

The development of a competency-based approach to theological education is a work in progress. As pioneers in the development of this approach, we have struggled to know when would be the best moment to "write it up." At certain points, our writing has felt premature—like we were trying to lock onto convictions that were still up for debate. At other points, we felt like we were a little late—writing things that are already well and deeply understood. With that acknowledged, we would encourage you as the reader to take this for what it is worth. We felt that, at some point, someone needed to get these ideas into print with the hope that the movement can spread. We thought, why not us?

Together, we represent a little bit of diversity and a lot of homogeneity. We operate on different sides of the US–Canadian border. Our personal styles and approaches to life are very different. That said, we are both white males operating within a broadly evangelical perspective. Our schools are not large by the standards of higher education—although, as we write this, they are growing quickly. Since Greg's school, Kairos University, adopted these principles and practices, it has experienced dramatic growth, leading to partnerships and iterations all around the world and the launch of a university, which he now leads. Kent has gone through this journey twice, first at the seminary where he taught and led for twenty-five years (Northwest Seminary and College), then subsequently at another school (Providence University College and Theological Seminary), where he has been able to apply these principles not only in a seminary environment but in a university, engaging all the breadth that such an opportunity offers.

While we have come to agree on what we are presenting in these pages, we first developed our thinking independently, then honed our ideas through years of dialogue and collaboration both personally and institutionally. That is who we are. We look forward to seeing how these thoughts will shape the ideas of others who come from broader perspectives than what we represent.

We encourage you to treat this work as you would any other. Read with an appreciative but critical eye. Translate freely into your own interests and idioms. Take what is useful to you and feel free to jettison the rest—just not too quickly. The ideas we present are challenging to conventional opinions of higher education. While we don't expect you to buy into every point, we hope that some of what we write will leave a mark. Theological education is overdue for renovation.

We recognize that we are working within the broader framework and movement known as competency-based education (CBE). Having contributed to this larger field, we are well aware of the breadth of understanding attached to this language. Many have rejected competency-based methodologies because they sense these approaches are too concerned with efficiency and overly impressed with application. We believe that if you give us a chance, you will find that we have the same concerns. Much that passes for CBE amounts to nothing more than mechanized learning, which atomizes outcomes into discrete competencies so that they can be checked off with haste. It often seems as though such programs have enrollment growth and fast completion of programs as their goals. In these cases, CBE is little more than a volume business that treats learners like widgets and outcomes like commodities.

This is far from our conception of what is possible. We hope that the thoughts in this book might help to steer the dialogue around CBE and CBTE toward a more productive end.

Competency-based theological education is an approach to education in which learner formation is rooted in contextualized standards of excellence, shaped by the recognition that the act of knowing requires the integration of content, character, and craft, and evaluated in the context of team-based mentoring. Therefore, learner progression is marked by the observable demonstration of integrated knowing rather than by time, input, or curricular stages. Furthermore, quality is measured by learner outcomes rather than assumed based on the path, resources, or people engaged in the formational journey.

A big part of this sort of project relates to establishing a lexicon. We appreciate that some of our terminology will be utilized differently by others within the field. This is normal for a subject that is still "wet cement." We ask that you seek to appreciate what we intend by the words we use. You can then interpret from within your own linguistic construction. Perhaps this book will help to build some consensus around the language.

We have tried to write collaboratively, in keeping with our ideas about education. Our process was for one of us to write a chapter, then have it shaped and edited by the other. Kent wrote the first draft of the various "principles," and Greg wrote the first draft of the "practices." We each wrote some of the "proposals" and collaborated on the first chapter. Careful readers will readily discern the differences in style. There is some overlap. We are okay with that.

Our hope is that these thoughts will fan the flame. We look forward to your responses. We especially look forward to seeing fresh expressions of theological education for the good of the church and for God's kingdom.

CHAPTER 1

A PROBLEM WITH
THEOLOGICAL EDUCATION

There is a fresh movement of the Spirit sweeping through theological education. Competency-based theological education (CBTE) represents one of the most exciting and innovative expressions of our work in recent years. God is doing amazing things through the church for the life of the world, and theological education continues to be a vital aspect of that work. Stories of God's provision, the work of the Spirit in the lives of people, and the redemptive love found in Jesus Christ abound throughout seminaries and theological schools around the world. Agencies like the Association of Theological Schools (ATS), the Association for Biblical Higher Education (ABHE), and the International Council for Evangelical Theological Education (ICETE) bear witness to the global reach of our work for the good of people and to the glory of God. We are proud of our engagement with these groups and with the schools they represent. Our enthusiasm for our mutual achievement has not blinded us to a problem, however.

The problem to which we are referring is much deeper than the daily practices of an institution. It isn't about enrollment, finances, staffing structures, faculty arrangements, or the various other aspects of institutional life. While each of those may be addressed in the pages of this book, they are not, in our opinion, the fundamental issue. Rather the issue, challenge, or problem is that, somehow, over time, the church and the academy have grown apart.

Nearly every institution of theological education can trace its roots to a time when it was founded "by the church and for the church." That is to say, a group of people felt it was necessary to develop leaders for churches that were rooted in a particular theological tradition, ministry practice, or ministry context. To solve that real challenge, they formed a school that would be focused on that work. Over time, that deep connection or shared mission began to fade. Schools and churches began to see each other differently—one leaning toward pragmatism and one toward theological depth. As a result, both began to feel a responsibility to balance the other, thereby creating more and more space between them. Schools tended to assume the role of "prophet," and their voice became profoundly shaped and formed by the traditions and practices of the academy more so than by the life and work of local communities of faith.

In this context, the church tended to assume the role of "leadership developer," and the church's voice became profoundly impacted by the traditions and practices of corporate America. While some might suggest that this focus on the practices and values of the business world was productive to some degree, the problem deepened as we let the corporate world dictate our measures for success. We began to value and pursue production-oriented leaders instead of stewarding followers of Jesus who in turn do the same.

In short, the values, organizational structures, approaches to human development, and academic designs utilized by seminaries and churches have become disconnected from the other's and have more in common with the world around them than the kingdom of which they are a part. While this has taken place over centuries, the distance between the two has grown at an accelerating rate since the mid- 1960s. In the 1960s, a group of financial experts led by Warren Deem was commissioned by the ATS to analyze graduate theological education. His team discovered four primary challenges:

- Declining learner enrollment
- Reduction in learner to faculty ratio
- Small average size of seminaries
- Increasing costs per learner[1]

Many schools today express the same challenges. These stressors have only increased pressure on theological schools over the last several decades.

Dan Aleshire notes that schools in financial stress tend to make decisions by triage: we have focused on those things that are urgent more than those things that are important.[2] In the midst of challenge, the academy has tended to focus on survival—our mission has been to continue existing. Granted, that push toward survival is connected to a deeply felt impulse to maintain a prophetic voice in the body of Christ, to protect the integrity of the various academic disciplines, and to sustain the great tradition of the church. Unfortunately, in practice, survival has meant focusing squarely on increasing, or at least maintaining, enrollment and securing funding for steadily increasing budgets. In short, survival has meant trying to find new ways to sell a product.

While this was happening in seminaries, local churches were faced with very real challenges of their own. With a rapidly changing culture and generations of Christians pushing against the

---

1   Chris A. Meinzer, "Sustainability and Strategic Thinking in Theological Education," *In Trust Magazine*, Autumn 2019, https://www.intrust.org/Magazine/Issues/Autumn-2019/Sustainability-and-strategic-thinking-in-theological-education.

2   Daniel O. Aleshire, *Earthen Vessels* (Grand Rapids: William B. Eerdmans, 2008), 89.

modernist tendencies of the academy and the institutional church, the decentering of the church's voice in public discourse, and a dramatic demographic shift, churches have also tended to focus on survival. In a similar tinge approach to crisis management, *survival* has meant increasing or at least maintaining membership, as well as securing funding for steadily increasing budgets. There is no small irony in that our response to financial stress leads to the need for even more funding. This is what happens when we look to production-oriented leaders: we create a system that always needs more money.

As a result, we believe that today there is a vast divide between the local church and the institutions that were founded to develop leaders for those very churches. In many ways, this divide has been the result of pragmatic responses to very real challenges. On one hand, the academy has been striving to maintain a particular place and voice in ecclesiological systems. On the other hand, the church has been wrestling with what it means to exist in post-Christendom. The schools are begging to be heard by the churches, who themselves are trying to be heard by the world. In both cases, we are preoccupied with questions of survival rather than mission. Instead of asking, "How do we develop servants who are faithful citizens of God's kingdom?" we ask questions like, "How do we get more learners/members?" or, "How can we fund our budget?" Churches and schools are offering the same solutions to the same questions about the same problems, and, even then, we fail to hear each other. Preoccupied with our own concerns, the distance between the church and the academy has continued to grow.

The church knows that it needs leaders, but it is looking past the academy. Today, the majority of leaders in a local church have not engaged in conventional, accredited theological education. In fact, Justo Gonzalez notes that "in the entire picture of theological education in North America, ATS-style theological education is no longer normative."[3] Whether real or merely perceived, there is

---

3   Justo L. Gonzalez, *The History of Theological Education* (Nashville: Abingdon, 2015), 137.

widespread belief that theological education is disconnected from the life and ministry of local churches. That has been the case for decades and has led many to see the conversations happening in seminaries to be "an utter irrelevance to the life, worship, and mission of the church."[4] While it is true that people once thought it was necessary to attend seminary in order to be a leader in a vocational ministry setting, those times are past. "People doubt the value of a liberal arts or seminary education."[5]

Of course, we have all heard this refrain many times. There is nothing new to this critique. This is a problem much deeper than curriculum or pedagogy. We are dealing with a broken relationship—the blame for which can be shared equally. Just as churches have ignored the academy, the academy has looked past the church.

In our efforts to maintain our institutions, we in the academy have developed a mission of our own. That mission, while fully rooted in an honest desire to support the work of the church, has not been fully integrated into the life and ministry of local expressions of faith. Instead, we chase degree programs that we think have a market for enrollment. Rather than responding to the body of Christ, we respond to the things we think will bring in the most learners and money. As institutions, we have largely overlooked the church's call for disciples who can lead others on mission. We have instead assumed a posture of certitude, in which we proclaim that we know what "they need" and work hard to provide programs that deliver those outcomes. It should not surprise anyone that our results have been poor.

Our point is that theological education is part of the Great Commission to make disciples. In almost every case, our schools were formed to help the body of Christ pursue that mission. More than servants of the church, we are part of the work of the church. Theological education flows from the life and work of the body of Christ. In our attempts to sustain local churches, build schools, and

---

4   Alister E. McGrath, *The Renewal of Anglicanism* (London: SPCK, 1994), 152.
5   Kevin Vanhoozer, "Learning Christ: Theological Education for Theological Discipleship" (paper, Karam Forum, Trinity Evangelical Divinity School, Deerfield, IL, 2017), 1.

survive cultural and institutional crises, we have failed to foster a deep and collaborative relationship. We have failed to listen to one another in our mutual desire to "succeed."

We would be careful to say that competency-based theological education is not the only solution to the problems we describe. There are many who are providing other creative and meaningful ways of addressing these concerns. We celebrate all of it. We also believe that CBTE is particularly well suited to offer something meaningful in response to these challenges.

A significant problem with theological education is that it is often separated from the local church. The time has come for that to change. We want to rebuild the relationship between the academy and the church. We believe competency-based theological education offers a powerful way forward because it helps bring focus back to our mutual mission, which is stewarding followers of Christ who flourish in their vocations for the sake of the world.

THE PRINCIPLES OF
COMPETENCY-BASED
THEOLOGICAL EDUCATION

Competency-based education is about developing demonstrated capacities in people so that they can faithfully engage the challenges and opportunities present in their contexts. This is to say that CBE exists for a purpose outside of itself.

COLLABORATIVE MISSION

Mission, as a concept, suggests that there is something in the world that is worthy of focused action. But the change we want to see will not happen on its own. Change requires the intentional action of people who are prepared and capable to engage in the faithful activities required. People like this are not readily available. They need to be called forward and developed. They need to be stewarded.

The best educators understand that they are called to more than mere instruction—that there is a ground-level mission at the end of the process. They know that they are preparing people to better understand the world so that they can work alongside the Spirit as God transforms the world. Education must have a sense of the end to which it serves. Effective education is oriented toward a purpose—a mission.

Mission matters. The question is, whose mission? Most schools have a reasonable sense of what it would look like for them to be successful. Sometimes we even write these things down in some sort of mission statement. We know what we want. The problem is that if the school is focused on how it sees the world, it is going to have to promote that vision to others in order to achieve its intended potential. That's why we have marketing departments. We believe in what we are doing, but we appreciate that others might not see things from the same perspective, and so we have to sell them on it. Sometimes this strategy works.

But what if we were to de-emphasize our sense of mission in favor of the mission of the ones we hope to serve? Could we imagine aligning our mission with their mission so that our success is wrapped up entirely in theirs? Another way of posing this question is to ask, Who is your customer? Typically, people who run schools would say, Learners. We offer our products to individual people who will consent to let us influence them in the manner we prescribe.

Competency-based schools might have a different answer. They might say that their customer is the mission-holder—the employer, agency, or church that is already on mission and that needs well-prepared people to help them pursue that mission. They might describe a learner, but only if such learners do not see themselves as consumers of the educational product but as mission-holders themselves. The mission of the school, then, is the mission in the world, held by agencies and individuals who are driven by the change they want to see. Education is not the end in itself. Education is the means to some greater missional objective, and that objective is in the world before it is in the school. And that greater missional objective goes beyond some professionalized sense of ministry. We are not aiming for some form of "hyper-professionalization." It is that we must be in partnership with others.

If mission matters, then collaboration matters also. The world is a big place, and its need is larger than any individual could meet. Individual leaders succeed only when they can bring others to share their sense of mission. Schools succeed when they can lend their strength to that of others closer to the front lines of the needed action. Unless we collaborate with the mission-holder, our work will be stunted. We need their help to be sure that our work is grounded in reality and useful to the expected change.

The mission of theological education is the mission of the church, which is why competency-based *theological* education is such a worthy enterprise. Churches and their related ministries and agencies are about the work of making God's kingdom known. Seminaries and theological colleges can serve that same kingdom mission, but only as they collaborate with the church.

The particular focus of the school is the development of leaders who can demonstrate the competency to pursue productive missional ends. This is the *C* in CBTE, and it is a noble task. We prepare people who are competent for the purposes the church intends. The *T* in CBTE comes when we appreciate how the development of leaders fits into the larger calling of the Christian church.

The church is the instrument that God promised to bless for the work of his kingdom. You will not find reference to any seminary in the Scriptures. But by collaborating with the mission of the church, theological educators find their own mission. Our purpose is their purpose. When the church succeeds, the seminary can celebrate. It is a collaborative mission.

This collaboration is going to require a paradigm shift on the part of the seminary but also on the part of the church. Churches have become skeptical of seminaries, and seminaries have returned the favor. Seminaries are prone to believe that they have the answer for the church and, sometimes, perhaps they do. But churches find this to be condescending, all the more so when the seminary's answer seems out of touch with the mission on the ground. Many of us remember a time when the collaboration was unquestioned. Some of us even have a direct denominational connection written into our incorporating documents. But trust has been broken, and the road back to our remembered histories has become difficult to travel.

It has become common for churches to bypass seminaries and theological colleges, "growing their own" without access to the resources offered by schools. The schools themselves have begun looking past the church, offering their product directly to the self-selecting learner who may or may not have their call affirmed by anyone who knows the ground. Churches, desperate for the human resources demanded by their voracious sense of mission, are hiring people wherever they can find them, often without adequate background or preparation. Schools, responding to their own financial challenges, are pursuing alternative markets, finding new avenues of training that may or may not find connection with the mission of the church. Both parties need the other but, like ships in the night, they pass each other, speaking different languages and even flying different flags.

There is a tremendous opportunity for schools that can make the required shift. There is much to be gained by the school that can regain the confidence of the church. If we could recapture this vision, we could join with the fresh movement of the Spirit. But there is a trick to this reality, and it is wonderful: winning the trust of the church can only happen as we show them that we truly have a heart to walk alongside and serve them. Our self-interest will be met only by surrendering our selfishness. (This sounds profoundly theological. Perhaps a theological school might be able to manage it!) By putting the interests of the church and learner in front of the interest of the school, we will find, to our delight, that we discover an elevated purpose. If we can show ourselves to be honest about this, we will find it meets our every need.

This, then, is about developing a true service mindset. By placing others before ourselves, we collaborate with the mission-holder in the development of the people who can help it flourish in its callings. As a result, happily, we find we have achieved our mission in the bargain, but only to the degree that we serve. Could we do this? Could we humble ourselves to this degree? There are some specific questions we might want to face. We will look at each in turn:

1. Could we be willing to put everything into the service of the church's participation in God's mission?
2. Might we be willing and able to articulate our value to the church without denigrating theirs?
3. Would we be willing to let the church drive the process?
4. Would we be willing to make the first move?

Could we be willing to put everything into the service of the church's participation in God's mission? "Everything" is a big ask. We are talking about our brands, our strategies, our resources, our people. . . . Could we imagine marshaling all of what we are and represent, and framing that around the mission that the church is called to pursue?

If we could, some wonderful things could result. Kent recalls a pivotal moment in the conversation between his seminary and denomination. The rhinoceros in the middle of the room was a long-standing sense of distrust within the churches of the seminary faculty. It's not that there was no appreciation for the faculty or their work. Things were fine on a personal level, but the ivory-tower perception was well entrenched. Offhand comments would convey the pastor's sense that while faculty might know how to parse a Greek verb, they might also be out of touch with realities on the ground in church life.

But slowly, as the seminary showed that it was serious about serving and as the conversation continued, trust began to grow, coming to a head at a significant meeting of the faculty with the chief director of the denomination. At that meeting, the denominational leader offered a word of apology to the faculty on behalf of the churches, speaking to years of unappreciation and neglect of the voice that faculty could offer to the larger group of churches. This moment unlocked an opportunity for the faculty to find a renewed sense of its voice among the churches. That apology was reciprocated, as trust found a footing among those groups. It was this deep spiritual work that opened the door for a powerful new opportunity for collaboration within these groups.

This story would not have happened if the denominational leader had not been willing to offer this apology. But it also would not have gotten anywhere if the faculty had not shown the same resolve to share some of its power within the educational process with the churches. When faculty exercises that power in a way that is disconnected from the church, an unintended consequence is that the church can lose confidence in the process, especially where faculty cannot express a meaningful connection to or appreciation for the work of the church.

This can be true even for faculty who have a history in church leadership. Kent was a pastor for eleven years prior to joining the faculty at his seminary. That experience lent him a lot of credibility in the first few years of his teaching work. But that pastoral "street cred" didn't have the long-term staying power that he might have wished. Academic life, at times, has a way of reducing, over time, the effect and quality of a teacher's pastoral experience.

A CBTE system addresses this situation by encouraging faculty and the church to share authority. When faculty members see that sharing authority is not a reduction of authority, amazing things are possible. CBTE faculty are as empowered as any, but they share that power with the church so that both voices are heard equally and powerfully within the system, for the benefit of both the learner and the church's mission.

We know that seminaries have concerns about the church. We see their warts even better than we see our own. We know that faculty want to speak that prophetic voice into the church. We want to fix them, and perhaps we could if we could only remove that troublesome log from our own eyes first. We are talking about our pride, and pride is the essence of every sin.

The truth is, we have very little to lose in this. It's not like theological education is a thriving industry. We have everything to gain if we could only believe that the power of a biblical humility, grounded in a theological conviction to look to the interest of others in the manner of Jesus, is the most powerful stance that we could take (Phil. 2).

Might we be willing and able to articulate our value to the church without denigrating theirs? We do have value. Our schools are rich in theological heritage and exegetical know-how. We engage in deep reflection on themes that matter, even if we seem to be a bit removed. We can help pastors and leaders understand their times by revealing lessons from the history of the church. We can bring research to bear in ways that might just make a critical difference on the ground. More than that, we have experience working with learners. We can help a person think, and sometimes it is that reflective thought that can empower a missional intention far beyond what might be possible from the seat of one's pants.

Could we find ways to share this with the church without making it seem like we are looking down on them? Sure, the church is often under-reflective. Of course, the church sometimes offers responses that are a little undercooked. So does the academy. The church wasn't perfect even in the Bible—why would we expect it to be any different today? If we could get past our snootiness and remember that we are the church, maybe we could learn how to be helpful to each other again. If we could prove to the church that our interest is in helping them develop their people in the competencies that matter to them on the ground, we might find ourselves getting somewhere.

Would we be willing to let the church drive the process? This one might be a little tougher for us. We are used to driving our own bus and flying our own flag. But perhaps we could find a deeper strength by letting the church take the lead. They could increase, while we could decrease, and in so doing we might find a more profound and productive competency of our own. Incredible things can be accomplished when we don't care who gets the credit.

We have found that collaborative, competency-based programs in theological education flourish when the collaborative agency takes good hold and learns to drive. When the mission-holder is unable to grow into this maturity, their programs tend to shrivel. *Would we be willing to make the first move?* This one should be easier if we have truly adopted a servant heart. If we care enough to serve, we will take the awkward step of reaching out to potential collaborators. We will risk the potential embarrassment of rejection. They might not believe us—at least not until we've shown them that we mean what we are saying. That will never matter to a servant, who will risk anything for the sake of those they serve.

In business, there is the idea of a "first-mover advantage," which suggests that in a disruptive environment the one who moves first receives the biggest potential advantage, and there might be some truth for us in this. If ever there was an environment ripe for disruption, it is theological education. But perhaps we are speaking here of a first-mover disadvantage—a purposeful disadvantaging of ourselves in the interest of our potential partners. This is always what a servant does.

Collaborative mission is a cornerstone principle of competency-based theological education. It is the embrace of the mission of the church by the heart of the servant, so that the kingdom comes on earth as it is in heaven.

CONTEXTUAL DISCIPLESHIP

The best place to learn how to lead the church is in the church. This might sound like we are stating the obvious, except for the fact that it has been forgotten by those of us who treat the church as an afterthought. If the mission of the seminary is the mission of the church, we would do well to consider the resource the church offers in the training of its own leaders.

In fact, one might say that leadership development is the job of the church. The fact that it was contracted out to seminaries for the last number of centuries does not counter the fact that the calling out and raising up of gifted leaders is biblically assigned to no one but the church. There are no seminaries in the Scriptures. Perhaps one could point to Paul's Syrian exile in Galatians 1, but even that was not presented as a prototypical model for absolving the church of its responsibility.

It just makes sense. Context is how we learn just about everything in life. For years we have asked learners to tell us how they learned to operate their computers or their cell phones. Did they learn by reading the manual or by just messing around with it? In every single case, across cultures and countries, decades and demographics, the answer is the same: almost everyone learns to do things by doing things. (Well, there's always one guy, but when pressed even he will admit that he starts by playing, but quickly reverts to the manual when he runs into difficulty. Don't we all?)

This is not to say that there is no value in understanding. "Incline your heart to understanding," says Proverbs 2:2 (NASB), but that advice is offered in the context of wisdom that has a deeper sense than mere content acquisition. Neither should it be lost on us that this is described as a matter of the heart. The heart learns by practice. Understanding shows itself by wisdom, through the insights gained by application.

Cognitive instruction matters. It is important that we can break down a subject to understand its importance. It matters that leaders can articulate their work with precision and a depth of intellectual understanding, though perhaps that importance has been a little overplayed. I am currently writing this paragraph on a computer that I barely understand. I could not take it apart and put it back together. My understanding around its fundamental principles is rudimentary at best. Yet, I am able to utilize the computer effectively and produce the result that I intend.

When it comes to the subjects favored for teaching in seminaries, we could have a lively debate. The classic example is the study of the biblical languages. Few seminaries would advocate for the full removal of biblical language study from their curriculum. But most pastors we know would say that they seldom use this capacity, even when they have learned it well—at least not in any profound manner. Some might argue, further, that the Greek and Hebrew they "learned" in seminary offered them just enough understanding to be dangerous. Few of them would say that they have confidence to challenge what is offered to them in commentaries.

There is a place for deep instruction in the biblical languages within seminary curricula, but is it true to assert that this is necessary for all? The advent of biblical software programs might press the question even further. Perhaps it might be wiser if we focused our work on helping learners to a place where they can confidently and effectively appreciate what the commentaries are offering, learning to utilize the software to a point of effectiveness, rather than trying to turn every learner into a first-class scholar of Koine Greek.

This is, of course, only an example, and a controversial one at that. Whether or not you agree as to the importance of Greek instruction, the point stands. Mere instruction in the languages or any other aspect of the seminary curriculum is no guarantee of learner success when measuring the effect of that learner's postgraduation ministry. We must do more than simply offer instruction.

Classrooms are efficient if content distribution is the goal. But if that were our objective, there would be better resources yet. Content is the easiest thing that we do as schools. Content is everywhere, especially in these days of digital dissemination. There is always going to be someone else who can offer content as good as yours in a manner that is cheaper, flashier, and more accessible than you are going to be able to do. If our priority is communicating content, then our business model is going to be a dicey proposition.

Of course, good educators have always understood that we aspire to more than that. We have all tried to market our classrooms as mentoring environments, but we would challenge the degree to which this noble intention has been achieved. Having taught in classrooms for decades, we have observed that actual mentoring in such contexts is rare. The numbers are against us. When the learner-to-professor count is higher than one-to-one, the bandwidth for discipleship just does not exist. When the structure of these settings is focused on critical engagement with our ideas, one cannot be confident about the results on the ground. The grades we award might be connected to some level of demonstrated ability to interact with content, but we have no means of measuring whether this has changed anything in life—and most research shows that the vast majority of content is not retained. We have too many stories of learners who excelled in the classroom only to crash in the church. We simply have to do better.

If our goal is wisdom, we need to take things further than our classrooms will allow. Understanding cannot be possible without real-life application. That being the case, perhaps it would be better if that is where we started. What if we started by valuing the various dimensions of knowing? Dan Aleshire notes, "If faculty act as if their intellectual ways of knowing are primary or superior to other ways, then students will be discouraged from pursuing some of the learning they need for effective service in the coming decades."[1]

The church needs leaders formed in the practices that produce faithfulness. The church and its affiliated ministries are looking for leaders who they can trust, who have proven their formation, their capacity to operate effectively outside of the mentoring situation. In short, they need to have been shaped as disciples and recognized as such by those whom they expect to follow them.

The mission of the church is about developing disciples for kingdom mission. If the church exists to make disciples, perhaps that should be the focus of its leadership development. The product of theological education must be a cadre of trusted disciples, capable of leading others in their train. What better place to develop them than the church?

This is not to say that the theological school has no place in the process—that we simply abdicate our roles. The reality is that the church has struggled to manage this mandate on its own. Schools and seminaries have tremendous value they can add. CBTE provides

---

1   Daniel O. Aleshire, *Beyond Profession: The Next Future of Theological Education* (Grand Rapids: William B. Eerdmans, 2021), 117.

a means by which it can be done. In partnership, theological schools, churches, and missional agencies can collaborate in the joint effort to develop the disciples needed to lead the church into its future. We will do this better together. Theological schools bring systems and structures that can support the intentions of the church within the culture and theological context of the church. Let us just be sure that these systems support the church's mission and not merely prolong the tired, institutional structures perpetuated by the schools.

There are several reasons why contextual discipleship matters. For one, the context provides a multimodal learning opportunity. Learners learn best when challenged by a variety of learning modes. Churches offer all of them. Not only can the learner find instructional opportunities, but the learner can put that instruction into immediate practice, testing learnings through engagement with real people in real time. In keeping with the idea of "competence," learners will show the level of their skill. If they do not yet have the goods, they will not be able to hide their deficiency. But the contextual process will provide the support the learner needs to rise to the challenge over time.

These contexts provide further opportunity for learners to be tested, not only on their proficiency of content and their skill but also on their wisdom and their character. The shape of a person will be noticed. They will not be able to hide the rough edges of their arrogance, their selfishness, or their fear. Character counts in the real practice of ministry, and it ought to count in the development of a disciple.

Contextual discipleship allows for longitudinal assessment. Developing a trustworthy disciple is going to require patience. Patience is possible in a contextual system that is not enslaved by a semester. In context, we can watch a learner over time. You might be able to fool us for a moment, but time always tells. Eventually we will see learners as they are.

But time also allows for development and deepening in the disciplines that matter. Mentors can be patient, knowing that leadership development is the long game. To quote Churchill, failure is never fatal. We can allow for the courage to continue over time. Context allows for time to be productive, as the learner has a venue to test and prove proficiency over the long haul.

Theological educators understand the importance of assessment. CBTE allows for an assessment process that is not arbitrarily measured. We can take our time. We can also be assured that we are not being fooled. Contextual discipleship is ensured by many eyes and observers, most of whom have the interests of learners at heart.

Contextual discipleship also allows for assessment to be viewed holistically. Theological schools have long appreciated the value of an interdisciplinary education. Unfortunately, understanding the conceptual value of such an ideal is different than delivering on it. The siloed nature of conventional education makes this challenge difficult. Contextual education, by contrast, can deliver this with confidence.

Contextual ministry requires learners to integrate their learning as a normal way of business. Ideas must be taught to others and proven over time both in craft and character. We can assess learners not only on the basis of what they have learned but also on the basis of their forming these things to good effect in others. In the classroom, assessors are limited to a narrow range of indicators. CBTE offers a much broader range of challenges and checkpoints, bringing a vast array of holistic data for assessment.

Contextual discipleship guarantees results consistent with the culture of the context. While we might not want to admit it, conventional education was built by Western white men, to produce more of the same. While we have been able to break out of some of those structures in more recent times, educating more and more women and people of various ethnicities, we are still replicating the ways enshrined by those who originally built our systems. The hegemony of the original design cannot be challenged without a breaking of the structures.

CBTE builds from the values important to the context. It is agnostic to the modality, allowing the ways and means of the context, wherever it is found, to be appreciated and utilized to the benefit of the church or agency anywhere in the world. Already, CBTE has taken root across the world, but not because it is yet another approach championed by the sanctioned custodians of education. Just the opposite. It is finding currency around the world precisely because those custodians are handing over the keys to the enterprise. Theological education will only truly embrace its global aspirations as the global contexts get to call the tune. Contextual discipleship, as a value, is singing that same song.

Competency-based theological education is about leading learners to develop and display the outcomes that matter within a given context. The disciples that are formed will match the culture on the ground and will possess the skill to read and adapt to new cultures and contexts, or to changes in their own. This is guaranteed as learners work within that culture to develop the things that matter. As learners display these qualities to the satisfaction of those assessors, mentors, ministry colleagues, and ministry recipients, together they all can celebrate the achievement of the desired result. As learners display these things, it is understood that others will be led to a similar display. Disciples multiply by nature. This is a system that honors that principle.

The mission of the church is to multiply disciples until God's kingdom comes on earth as it is in heaven. Leaders, then, must be disciples themselves. The best model for discipleship ought to be Jesus himself, who mentored the original twelve into a group that turned the world upside down. As they walked together, learned together, talked together, and practiced ministry together, they came to trust each other. All of it happened in the context of ministry.

CBTE has put structure to this system so that the manner of our training can be replicable and approved by accreditors. We have not improved on the discipling practices of Jesus. We have merely made them possible within the practices of higher education and for the good of the church and those who lead it.

INTEGRATED OUTCOMES

As Northwest was developing its first CBTE program, Kent had an early conversation about it with an ATS accreditation liaison. It felt like there was a lot at stake in that conversation. Many people had told them not to bother with accreditation, because it was felt that this would only get in the way. But they believed they would be able to go further if they had the backing of organizations like the ATS and so, with a little fear, they broached the conversation. Kent recalls the conversation like this:

> "We've heard for years from you that it's all about outcomes," Kent said. "We're going to find out if you really mean it." This wasn't meant to be an adversarial challenge. It was simple fact, and the response we received was more than we could have hoped for.
> "Of course, it is all about outcomes," the liaison said.
> "Then this is going to be a great experience," was our response, and it certainly has been.

It is all about outcomes. Competency-based theological education is driven by the identification of a set of integrated outcomes that become the end objective for learning. If the learner is able to demonstrate proficiency within the stated outcomes, then the program and, by extension, our schools can claim that we have met our mission.

Many years ago, Stephen Covey taught us to "begin with the end in mind," the second principle in his *The 7 Habits of Highly Effective People*.[2] CBTE programs honor that principle, through attention to backward design. By focusing on the "ends" we are able to avoid the trap of acting as if the structural interests of the institution are of greater concern than the mission of that same organization.

Institutions, over time, take on a life of their own. This is natural. As the institution grows and lengthens its life span, it becomes needy for itself. Where once the mission was at its heartbeat, in time the sustenance of the institution becomes the overarching end. Whatever energy the business or school can muster becomes focused more on those systems and interests that will keep the institution functioning. Ironically, this is a death spiral, as the institution be-

---

2   Stephen R. Covey, *The 7 Habits of Highly Effective People: Powerful Lessons in Personal Change* (New York: Free Press, 1989).

comes insatiable, requiring increasing amounts of energy simply to survive. The more the focus shifts to preservation, the faster the demise, and the more distant is the mission. This is where schools go to die. It can take a long time to kill a theological school all the way. These schools can continue to function in a kind of zombified existence, but their missional effectiveness will have been betrayed by an unhealthy focus on their own survival.

Few of us would see this in ourselves, but consider how things like faculty tenure, deferred building maintenance, and curriculum planning can each become important for its own sake, often at the expense of the learner's actual interest, or that of the churches and ministries we hope to serve. We believe that our marketing initiatives, campus planning, and fundraising projects are all in the interest of helping us do a better job of learner service, and that might even be something close to true. But if we were honest enough and courageous enough to actually put the end, the missional objective, ahead of our own interests, we might find that there are better ways to go. These are not easy issues to face, but we have found that there are efficiencies and opportunities that might be more compelling if we truly put the outcome in the driver's seat.

While this is true of our institutions, it is also true of our work with learners. Learners are quick to learn the unspoken secret that they will be measured mostly on their capacity to jump through our hoops and tick our boxes, realizing that graduation might not be much more than proving the capacity to persevere. Yes, that might be an exaggerated statement, but maybe not by much. How much better would it be if we could show learners that they will be measured entirely by the degree to which they can discern, develop, and demonstrate proficiency of the outcomes we all claim to care about?

This might be a good place to note that not all competency-based programs are equal, either in their intent or their effect. There are some well-known CBE programs that, in our estimation, tend to lean toward box-ticking. These programs tend to break outcomes down into atomized competencies that can be readily achieved and affirmed. This approach allows learners to quickly progress through a larger program, proving their capacity to handle a diverse set of challenges and opportunities. While such a system may work in some situations, it tends to be an inadequate approach to integration and formation. Such things are not reducible to component parts. The whole is always greater and more nuanced than the sum of its parts.

In competency-based *theological* education, we are concerned about developing all of the soft skills and character aspects that attend to a learner's emotional intelligence and spiritual formation. These are things that do not easily fit into tick-able boxes. These are things that must be observed over time by mentors who are looking not only for efficiencies but also for the depth that will allow us to trust the learner.

The goal, as we will say repeatedly, is to get the learner to the place where we can "trust them in the wild" without close supervision. We want to be able to believe in the learner, not just because she can do the things that must be done but because she will be the person that she must be. We are trying to lead learners to more quickly attain the qualities of wisdom and experience that help them know what to do and why. When we see it, we trust it, and trust is the essence of assessment within all CBTE programs.

One of our mentors is a long-time veteran on a significant university faculty. When he joined our CBTE faculty, he admitted to some skepticism. But when it came to graduating his learners a few years later, his tune had changed. "I've been hooding graduates for thirty years," he said. "Usually, I have done this act *hopefully*, but this is the first time that I have done it *confidently*, knowing that every one of these graduates has the stuff they need to flourish." He was saying that he could trust these learners because he was able to see what they could do, and who they could be, before we let them walk the stage at graduation. When we get to this level, our collaborating churches and employers will trust our learners, and we will all flourish as a result.

Developing a robust set of integrated outcomes will require us to engage in close conversation with the churches and agencies that are serving in local communities. What would the mission-holding church, denomination, business, or agency describe as their desired outcome for the people they engage? What would it look like for us to describe a leader who we would be willing to trust in the wild without close supervision? It will be difficult for a faculty or school to determine this on its own. We need to be in deep dialogue with appropriate practitioners and other voices outside the walls of the seminary to craft a robust recipe.

That kind of conversation might be difficult. There is a lot of accumulated distrust between churches and their seminaries. Some of that concern has been well earned. We may, in fact, be blind to the ways that we have earned enmity along the way. Sometimes there needs to be words of apology and repentance for the arrogance and contempt we have had for one another.

There were some moments like that for us as we were building programs—beautiful moments, like the one mentioned earlier, when faculty and denominational leadership came together in repentance and prayer for the years when we had not seen the best in one another. The tears shed put us in a good place to imagine a better future together.

We do not have to be concerned that this kind of collaborative effort will result in outcomes that are purely pragmatic. Most of us could do with a lot more pragmatism in our programming, of course. This is not something that we need to fear. In fact, we have found that the churches and denominations that we serve are just as interested in deep reflection as our faculties are. One amazing moment comes to mind, when faculty met with denominational leaders to confirm the final form of our competency-based curriculum.

"We are wondering whether there is enough biblical exegesis in the program," said one of the denominational leaders, causing the tenured New Testament faculty member at the table to gasp in surprise.

"You mean we could have more?" he asked, the possibility alive in his eyes.

"Of course," the leader said. "You know that we care that our leaders are competent with the Scriptures as well."

And of course, they do. Our partners want the best leaders they can have. In those rare cases where the faculty have an objective that is not shared by the partners, the door is opened for a critical conversation. In our experience, that conversation is good for both sides. The goal is to write a set of integrated outcomes that best describe a mature follower of Jesus—not solely in terms of what work the learner does, but in terms of who the learner can become and what she or he becomes capable of. The word "outcome" describes the specific, tangible result embodied by the successful learner. It is narrower than the overall *program objectives* but broader than the specific *competencies* or *indicators of proficiency*. Those indicators of proficiency are more discrete, recognizable aspects of the larger outcome. They might be cognitive abilities connected to content, specific skill sets, or observable character traits, but together they describe an outcome that is integrated. Without this level of integration and holistic assessment of the learners, competencies function like widgets—measurable and manageable learning chunks that can be checked off as they are completed. In theological education, we are trying to see the process in a more integrated manner.

There are no aspects of proficiency for ministry leadership that do not require theological acumen, biblical rootedness, practical skill, and proven character. A well-designed outcome will find a place for all four. This won't always be overt in the writing of the highest-level description, but when the outcome with its indicators, inputs, and interactions are all taken as a whole, each of these aspects will be fully expressed.

Take the following outcome example, derived from Northwest Seminary's CBTE MDiv program:

> CBE 504: Shaped by Scripture
> Learners express a personal commitment to, relationship with and love for God which is fed by their ongoing growth in their knowledge of Him through biblical exegesis, theological understanding, and devotional reflection applied in ministry and life.

In this high-level outcome description, the interest is to ensure that learners are personally shaped by a deep engagement with the Scriptures. Note that the learner is expected to demonstrate relational love for God, fed by or deriving from their demonstrated skill or practical capacity in the exegesis of Scripture and the resultant theological understanding. This integrates all four interests without compromise. This, then, will be clarified and detailed in a fuller set of indicators, interactions, and inputs.

This kind of development is where the gravitational pull of conventional education becomes particularly challenging. We are so accustomed to breaking out curriculum according to our siloed disciplines. We seem to believe that the way to protect quality as it applies to biblical or theological studies is to keep disciplines distinct from one another, in the concern that integration necessarily requires some level of dilution or compromise.

But this is to misunderstand the very nature of the word. *Integration* has at its root concepts like integrity, which describes structural wholeness. In mathematics, we speak of an *integer*, which is a whole or non fractional number. When we integrate things like exegesis and theology, we are combining their interests without compromising their fundamental characters. We might argue, further, that this is to treat the two most appropriately. To isolate exegesis is to diminish its power and intention. To try to derive theological truth without its biblical foundation will only lead to problems. To do either without an interest to their consequences on the ground, or without attention to the impact on human character, is to damage the fundamental nature of these concerns. The character of theological education drives toward this integration, even if our academic structures have struggled to embody it.

When CBTE programs integrate all four aspects—theological acumen, biblical rootedness, practical skill, and proven character—we improve the quality of our work. A few years ago, we were in conversation with a faculty member from one of the largest competency-based university programs in the world. "We're pretty good at content delivery," he said, "and we are very good at assuring skill development. But we are nowhere when it comes to character, and character is everything." He meant his comment to compliment the way that we have been able to integrate all of these interests in our understanding of competency-based *theological* education. This is what puts the "T" in CBTE.

Character is the hardest part, but character is everything, because character is all about trust. If you don't have trust, you don't have much. If we want graduates that people can have confidence in, we are going to have to go the distance.

We understand the size of this "ask." We are demanding a lot more of ourselves than what we had previously aspired to accomplish. It would be so much easier if we could be happy to ensure that our learners were merely well informed or that they had their theological statements all in order. Failing that, a reliable set of skills seems like it ought to be enough. But it will never be enough until we know that we can trust the person who demonstrates those skills.

It's not that we have not understood this. We have described it as *formation*. It is just that we did not have effective tools to achieve it. We can remember the days when seminaries and theological colleges tried to attend to formation by means of residential life or through things like chapel services. These days, few learners live on our campuses. Even if we can get our learners to our chapels, it is a lot of weight to place on that single practice as a method of assuring character. Even still, residential life and chapels did not produce an on-the-ground type of formation because it was created in an alternate reality, one separated from the day-to-day life of the local church.

We believe that the kind of contextual mentoring process we are describing is capable of this expanded expectation. It starts with aiming at the right end. If we can begin with an end that anticipates the formation not just of a graduate but of a disciple, we will be getting where we need to go.

Psalm 78:72 describes our integrated objective in the person of King David: "With upright heart he shepherded them and guided them with his skillful hand" (ESV). It is with this combination of heart and hand that we can change the world. This is the outcome for which we aim.

CUSTOMIZED PROFICIENCY

Some of our competency-based programs result in the award of a master of divinity degree. It has long been a joke in theological education that one might actually be able to master the divine, but of course it is less a matter of mastering God than it is to be mastered by him. The outcomes we pursue are actually callings. God leads his people to serve him in his kingdom. Our objective is to lead people to the places where they can reliably serve, in keeping with the callings they have received from God.

Proficiency,[3] of course, is a lot to ask. Complete proficiency might have to wait for heaven. In the meantime, we pursue a kind of "reasonable proficiency," which speaks more to a sense of trustworthiness. We are looking to lead people to the places where we could trust them to fulfill their callings without close supervision. Think about a violinist in the symphony—perhaps not having the level of first-chair virtuosity, but competent and technical, with the capacity to deliver with heart and with excellence. Think in terms of a craftsman who might not be commissioned to build the furnishings for Buckingham Palace but whose work might be cherished in your home or mine. These are people who know what they need to know, which means they can do what they need to do and are who we need them to be. They are proficient in content, character, and craft—the three dimensions of knowing.

Customized proficiency is, then, another of the principles inherent to CBTE. This is governed, as we have said, by stated outcomes—the markers of their discipleship are determined in collaboration with the context. These are the fixed targets. These are the pieces in which we expect proficiency to be demonstrated.

But learners vary in their capacity, and contexts differ in what

---

3   In the early days of CBTE, we tended to speak about *mastery model learning*, which was a commonly understood expression in the world of higher education. With greater sensitivity to the negative connotations of the word *master*, we have chosen to use the word *proficiency* instead.

they demand. We tend to imagine learners arriving as relatively blank slates. We usually design our curriculum to lead learners through a standardized and comprehensive program of studies that assumes they know nothing and can do little when they first come to our attention. While a comprehensive approach is wise, we might do better to appreciate the prior learning and capacity that learners bring with them when they come—particularly at the graduate level.

Some learners will be able to achieve proficiency of certain elements very quickly; others will take longer, though perhaps in some other area of study, that dynamic might be reversed. We remember one learner who came to our program with a great deal of experience. He had a particularly high level of competence in leading and managing small group systems. His expertise was evident by the fact that he had been invited to lead seminars for other churches, coaching those leaders in the development of their own programs. One of the competencies expected in this learner's program related to small group ministry, as this was important to the denomination we were serving. In this case, our learner was able to display proficiency of this outcome almost immediately. There was no point in requiring him to jump through our hoops and do the busy work required by the assignments for this outcome when his proficiency was already proven and visible to all.

CBTE systems allow learners to move at a faster pace when it comes to areas in which they have already demonstrated proficiency. Conventional programs require a one-size-fits-all demand asking that every learner has to grind out every piece, whether these various assignments are useful or necessary to the learner's display of proficiency. CBTE programs allow mentors to recognize proficiency more quickly, celebrating it and moving on to other areas of greater concern.

The capacity to customize learning is an essential element of a program with the goal of proficiency. This is the difference between means and ends. If our focus is on the ends—the outcome—then we should be able to get creative with the means. Part of the assessment of a learner will be to determine what means will be most effective in developing the learner's proficiency of discrete program elements. Best practice will mean that the learner is directed to focus energy on those areas that will be the most needed and most fruitful, instead of wasting time on those areas where the learner has already proven proficiency.

It may be, for example, that there is a better book for a particular learner than the one that has been assigned in the standard-set curriculum—or perhaps, a better project than mere book reading. Perhaps someone has produced an exceptional podcast on a subject that would be productive for a particular learner's specific need. That learner ought to be able to take advantage of that learning opportunity, whether or not it was produced by one of our faculty or included in our curriculum. Perhaps there is an unusual project or opportunity present within the learner's community that is unique both to the learner's ministry context and to his or her specific learning need. Our systems have to be built so that we can do that sort of thing without having to manipulate the fixed nature of the program.

Customization of learning is an important part of the CBTE experience. We are not turning out widgets or assembling cars along a line. Educators have long acknowledged the need to adjust teaching methods to better suit the variety of learning styles that learners present. This is a massive challenge for conventional education, which more often resembles an industrialized system of learner management.

Typically, the professor has come with a bundle of notes that will be shoehorned into the available time. Learner questions come as intrusions to a teacher who feels pressured to fit the material into the limited time frame allotted for the class. This system favors uniform learning, where the learner is expected to adjust to the system, rather than the other way around. There is a lot of human wreckage attending to these systems. Retention is a challenge, as high proportions of learners drop out and disappear, sometimes deeply scarred by the experience. This approach fits poorly with the values of a Christian education—especially when there is a better option.

We are talking about adaptive learning that builds from one learning opportunity to another along a pathway that can twist and turn, or even turn back upon itself when necessary. In a conventional program, when a learner delivers an assignment, we assess and grade it. If the learner has delivered B-quality work, that is what we give them and that is where the story ends. But what if we were able to say to the learner, "Let's try that again, only this time let's pay attention to this particular concern"? Is it possible, with a more flexible system that allows for more time and greater input, that we might be able to move that learner from B- to A-quality? In most cases, the answer would be yes, but only if the system would allow for that kind of customization. If the learner runs out of time because the learning system is held hostage by a semester-based calendar, then we might have to give up on our dream of proficiency.

This is particularly true of things like character development. If our goal is to lead learners to the place where they can be trusted to consistently act with grace and humility, we might need more than fifteen weeks to prove it.

Moving our curriculum toward proven proficiency will allow churches and agencies to place greater trust in our graduates. The system of credit hours and semesters is very convenient for keeping the machinery of academia in motion. Such things allow us to standardize, measure, and pay for our institutional structures—but they do very little for the learner or for the mission we intend to serve. There is little wonder that our self-promotion falls on increasingly deafened ears within the church.

There are, of course, many different vocational outcomes for the learners we intend to train. Even within a relatively closed system, like a particular denomination or a specific mission-holding agency, there could be a number of roles that a learner might fulfill. Our original thought was that we would need to write the standard-set curriculum many times over to meet the need of multiple vocational or learner-learning outcomes, even for a particular church application.

What we learned was that the general outcomes could be standardized more than what we had originally thought. It turns out that we didn't need to rewrite the entire set of outcomes for a youth pastor, a children's director, and a lead pastor. We found that all of that variation could be customized within the mentoring. All of these people needed the same broad outcomes, but the way those outcomes would be applied could be most helpfully addressed through the way the mentors adapted the material to the particular need and interest of the learner. We just had to make sure that there was that form of vocational expertise represented on the learner's mentor team. And we needed systems that could allow for these kinds of on-the-fly adjustments.

All of this variability sounds amazing at first, but the truth is, it can be daunting to be faced with this level of choice. It does require learners and mentors to be attentive to their self-assessment and understanding of their context. Sometimes following a well-defined path that offers little choice can be easier.

In the early days, McDonald's was careful to limit a customer's options. You could order a Big Mac, fries, and a Coke. There were other options, but they were not emphasized. Much of the exponential growth of the restaurant was due to the simplicity and the reproducibility of their offerings anywhere in the world. But that world has changed, and now there are a myriad of options that change from country to country. Ordering a McDonald's hamburger in Paris is very different than doing the same thing in New York. Now we stand in front of a digital board that allows us to choose everything down to the amount of tartar sauce we want on our Filet-O-Fish.

The capacity to customize is a standard feature of contemporary life. We just have to find ways to make it manageable. We are saying that the standardization of customization makes for better learning. Learners need to be given the tools to manage their learning at their own pace, according to their own need, and in their own manner. We also have to do this in a way that can be managed.

The management of customized learning requires a significant level of self-discipline on the part of the learner. Developing proficiency in self-discipline is, in fact, part of the learning journey itself. Some may find it difficult and stumble. But self-discipline is a fundamental skill when it comes to the practice of a life in ministry. If learners cannot be brought to proficiency of this aspect, then we will not be able to have confidence in their work. How much better to have a system that reinforces the practice of the ministry for which they are being trained, in the very manner that the learner learns?

Some of us are old enough to remember when young boys like us were referred to as "Master." There was a time when the term was used to politely address boys who were too young to be described as "Mister." This seems counterintuitive, given that proficiency tends to come with age. But perhaps there is something about a childlike faith that is a part of the process. Trustworthy graduates will be those who learn to be as children in their faith and in their learning process, growing toward maturity by the guidance of their mentors. These are the people whose leadership we will be pleased to follow. It is just that the path to get there might be winding.

TEAM-BASED MENTORING

Mentoring is the best way to learn anything. It's how we learned to use our computers. It's how we learned to drive a car. You might remember, like we do, white-knuckling the back roads while your father or mother tried to patiently explain the nuances of operating the family car. It's not common to think of one's parents as mentors, but that's exactly what the good ones do.

It is through mentoring, if we are wise, that we learn how to be parents ourselves, how to be married, and how to be disciples in Christ. We learn these things through patient observation, gentle correction, timely insight, and occasional rebuke. Sure, there are technical pieces we can learn through studying the manual, memorizing patterns, or passing tests, but we will learn better and more profoundly through the guidance, example, and encouragement of an experienced hand who cares enough to show us the ropes.

If this is true of mundane things like cooking and cleaning, it is definitely true of things like ministry leadership. The best way to learn how to lead a ministry is to walk with a ministry leader who has proven leadership capacity and who will be generous enough to share what they have learned for the benefit of others.

Best practice in competency-based theological education is to think more as mentors than as instructors. We need to think of ourselves more as encouragers than as assessors. Our work is more curating and customizing than it is informing and policing. By these means, learners can be led toward proficiency in ways that inspire and compel. When learning is formed in relationship, the lessons stick and the proficiency will last. Mentoring is relational learning, which is always going to be the most profound and effective means of deepening the understanding and capacity that we are looking for. It is always worth the investment it requires.

When we think about our own educational journeys, we remember the people who taught us more than the lectures they offered. We were far more deeply affected by the presence and character of those we sat with than the wisdom of their words. Often the most meaningful encounters occurred in the professor's office after hours, sitting together in the cafeteria, or in some other life encounter. Some of those people are still in our lives and continue to help us grow into the people they imagine for us.

Mentoring is about providing direction more than it is about providing information. Historically, theological schools have understood their role as providing expert content. Professors are those sages hired to provide wisdom by means of instruction. The lecture has been the gold-standard means of delivery, which is why infrastructure like classes, credits, courses, and semesters have made sense. But this is not the best way to lead a learner to proficiency of an integrated set of outcomes. It might not even be the best way to organize a school. If our schools are focused on the delivery of content, we are fishing in what could be called the "red ocean,"[4] a

---

4   "Red Ocean versus Blue Ocean Strategy," Blue Ocean, accessed June 13, 2023,

place of cutthroat competition. Good luck with that.

If we can learn to structure our schools so that we maximize our mentoring, we will be able to shape our offerings around the distinctive wisdom that only wise and experienced hands can bring. Mentors don't have to compete by showing that they know more or better than anyone else. By emphasizing mentoring, we are able to play to our strengths—the unique aspects of our lives and personalities that will truly set us apart. Mentors swim in the "blue ocean," a place of wide-open opportunity and possibility.

Not every professor will be good at this. Frankly, some teachers have never learned beyond the raw information of their subject. Some of our professors would have done well to have been mentored by someone trustworthy somewhere along the way. We will do well to choose mentors who get it, and who can show themselves to be effective in guiding their learners rather than simply instructing them.

CBTE allows mentors to imagine themselves as curators. In competency-based systems, mentors are not expected to be the world's leading expert on every subject. They are trusted, rather, to marshal their experience, their networks, and their critical thinking skills in ways that will be of best use to the particular needs of their learner.

Curation is contextual work. You would not expect to see the same exhibits at the Vancouver Art Gallery that you would find at Amsterdam's Rijksmuseum or the Metropolitan Museum of Art in New York City. If I am in Amsterdam, I expect to see the work of the Dutch artists. If I am in Vancouver, I expect to see West Coast aboriginal work—not exclusively, of course, but sufficient to reflect the specific interests of the region I am visiting. CBTE mentors curate the best, most useful resources and learning opportunities available to learners in their context, making use of the peculiarities of their place and learning from the specific challenges that their context offers.

The COVID-19 crisis offers an example. A pandemic is a con-

https://www.blueoceanstrategy.com/tools/red-ocean-vs-blue-ocean-strategy.

text, and it has been fascinating to help our learners learn from the unique challenges presented by this time of isolation. CBTE mentors make use of what the context gives them, be it a pandemic, a party, or a chance to preach. While the curriculum might offer a "standard set" array of assignments and expectations, mentors know how to take those materials and shape them uniquely for the learner. Perhaps a book should be swapped out for another reading that is going to be more productive for a specific learner. Perhaps a lesson would be better learned by another means. Mentors have the capacity to make those kinds of adjustments.

The best way to mentor is to work in teams. We have built all of our CBTE programs around the concept of multi-person teams, often consisting of a faculty mentor, an on-the-ground practitioner or vocational mentor, and a personal mentor—a third, big-picture person who may represent the broader network, denomination, or grouping that we serve or meet a personal need of the learner. Together, speaking with one voice, these teams work to direct, challenge, assess, and love the learner toward proficiency.

Each teammate brings something essential that none of them could offer entirely on their own. Mentor teams acknowledge that no one person can catch all the issues and bring all of the perspective necessary. Sure, the faculty mentor may focus primarily on academics and the vocational mentor on what the learner is doing in the ministry context, but that does not mean that they are uninterested in other things. Vocational mentors have a lot to offer in academic reflection, and most good academics will have some useful observations about application. By working in teams, we are able to broaden our coverage and lead the learner conversationally in a way that models the kind of relational ministry we would hope they could embody.

This is very different than the old internship model many of us have known. In the conventional approach to "field education," a faculty member oversees a learner's contextual engagement under the direction of a pastoral mentor in the field. Typically, that pastor is expected to send reports to the faculty member, who is very much in charge of the final assessment. In the end, it is the professor who gives the grade, even though they probably have had zero opportunity to actually observe the learner's work in context. The pastoral mentor, who has been there to observe, often "mails it in" (pun intended). The report they send offers marginal investment because she or he has very little stake in the academic grade. Do we need to point out how broken that system is?

By working together as teams, mentors have the ability to ensure a broader range of concern. The vocational mentor, present to the learner on an almost daily basis, is able to ensure that the learner has truly "got it." This mentor can observe how people respond to the learner's work and ministry and is available to see the display of the learner's character.

The faculty mentor is able to see these same things, although with a broader perspective. The faculty mentor can ensure that the learner is exposed to a world of experience beyond the confines of the context. Together, the team can ensure that the learner is fully and holistically prepared.

For this to work, the faculty mentor is going to have to embrace his or her role more as an integrationist than as a specialist. That is, their ability to integrate disciplines, to integrate theory and practice, and to integrate content, character, and craft will become their expertise. Traditionally, faculty increase in prominence by displaying competency as specialists within an academic discipline. In contrast, the CBTE system will value their contribution less for this specialized knowledge and more for their ability to lead learners to an appropriate level of critical thinking. We tell our faculty that we value them more for the fact that they have learned how to achieve specialization than for the content of their specialty. They are useful in the process because they have proven that they know how to think well. The challenge for them will be to help their learners gain the same capacity across the board. As curators of the learning experience, they can call in whatever disciplinary expertise might be needed for the benefit of the learner; they don't have to bear that expertise themselves. Their expertise lies in knowing how to recognize the needed knowledge and knowing where to find it. Faculty mentors are helping learners foster the ability to discern, develop, and demonstrate proficiency. We have discovered that there is significant value in having one faculty mentor work with a learner across the entirety (or most) of their program. Conventional theological education is highly siloed. Semester systems mean that faculty influence a learner for short, discrete seasons, usually three and a half months long. But this may not be long enough to truly see a learner change. Our faculty have found that they deeply enjoy the process of working with a learner over longer periods of time. This requires persistence and a deeper engagement. Longitudinal assessment can be challenging sometimes for academic people who are used to working with shorter (semester-based) periods of assessment. But we have yet to find a faculty member who has not grown to love this opportunity. Team-based mentoring turns out to be a real blessing. Our faculty report that they also appreciate the opportunity to work beyond the strict parameters of their disciplinary expertise. This kind of stretching must be done with caution and care, but it can be powerful for the learner. Rather than bouncing from one faculty member to another, these learners can grow through long-term, two-way investment with their chosen mentors.

There is a parallel challenge for the vocational mentor in this manner of teamwork. Practitioners are known to be activists. They tend to be independently minded. We have noticed that learners are attracted to mentors who have gained prominence through significant ministry accomplishment. There are times, however, when such people are not the most effective mentors. A vocational mentor has to be committed to the process and especially to the learner.

Often, when considering whether they will engage the process, a pastor will confess uncertainty around the time commitment required for mentoring. We try to gently remind them that the work of mentoring is actually the work of a pastor. Pastors typically have been among the first to criticize seminaries for being out of touch and for usurping the job of the church. We agree. The development of the next generation of leaders is the job of the church, and our experienced pastors are obligated to invest in those who will one day take their place. CBTE schools are giving these churches and ministries a means by which that can be managed and achieved.

In our experience, this integration of the world of the church and the world of the seminary has become very productive. It is a beautiful thing to see the synergy of these two worlds finding their way back to one another. It has been long overdue.

All of this will require humility on the part of the mentor team. Sharing the process and speaking with one voice can only happen when there is mutual respect on the mentor team. This might most significantly challenge the faculty mentor who is accustomed to being in the driver's seat in an academic world. Now the faculty member has to be willing to respect the voice of the practitioner as of equal value to his own. Likewise, the vocational mentor is going to have to set aside some prejudices. It could be messy, but it could also be beautiful. Is it possible that CBTE could be the means that brings the seminary and church back into appreciative dialogue with one another? In our cases, the answer has been yes.

We have seen some beautiful things along the way. In one such case, a learner called us twenty minutes after hearing of his father's unexpected death. We have taught thousands of learners over many years, but we have never had a learner from one of our conventional classrooms ever feel so invested in our relationship that they would call us in a moment quite like that. But this is the quality of relationship that can happen in a CBTE program when learners and mentors work together over time. It is a profound and wondrous thing. Now that learner is a CBTE mentor himself, sharing with another younger learner who is benefitting from his experience both as a CBTE student, but also now as a pastoral mentor.

CBTE programs are about creating an integrated process by which learners can both develop and display their proficiency of the outcomes that represent their callings. It employs a team of mentors who are going to be best positioned to assess whether that outcome has been achieved.

HOLISTIC ASSESSMENT

It is commonly held that you get what you measure. If you want to increase sales, you need to pay attention to your revenue numbers. If you want to lose weight, it is helpful to track related fitness goals. It might not be encouraging on any particular day, but consistent assessment of your achievement relative to a fixed target has a way of pulling you toward the intended result. When we have our eye on the target, it becomes easier to motivate ourselves to make that sales call or resist that piece of cheesecake. If we don't measure our progress, the goal becomes unfocused and unlikely.

Measuring also has a way of keeping us fixed on tangible results. An object could be ten or twelve inches in length, but it cannot be both at the same time. It is important to know which measurement is correct when the objective calls for precision. The contextual application will tell you what will be required. Assessing well ensures that the product you are shaping is fit for the intended task.

CBTE is essentially a system of assessment. We set targets and work with learners until they have developed and displayed their capacity relative to those targets. We measure constantly, and we notice when we are falling short. We take remedial action, constantly adjusting and consistently revising the process, until our assessment of the person matches the objective we are requiring. We mitigate the shortcomings and address the deficiencies. We know that growth will not happen without intentional action. Holistic assessment ensures that we keep our eye on the target. We believe that we will miss 100 percent of the targets that we fail to assess.

Holistic assessment is a lot to ask. The unexamined or only partially examined life is always easier. The learner will need to adopt a submissive spirit, showing a willingness to be assessed to a degree that might not be possible or even appropriate without consent. But the schools and agencies that run these systems must also submit themselves to assessing the effect of their own efforts. Poor learner performance might reflect more upon the school than it does upon the learner. To know the degree to which this might be the case is itself a reason to engage in robust assessment.

We understand the need to assess learners. We know that we need to take the measure of our learner's progress and achievement, but we might not always appreciate the breadth that this assessment must encompass. We need to monitor learner proficiency of content for sure, but we also need to assess the capacity to effectively pursue craft and to display the character necessary to lead within context. These three dimensions of knowing—content, character, and craft—must all be attended to when doing assessments. As Dan Aleshire put it, "Intellectual ways of knowing are not superior to these other ways of knowing."[5] Indeed, formation requires attention to multiple ways of knowing.

A lack of character can nullify one's proficiency of content or the quality of one's craft. Even learners of exceptional character might not be of much use if they cannot muster the necessary skill. It is hard to imagine that any competence in craft could be achieved without the requisite grasp of content or display of character. An effective assessment system must start with a biblical understanding of knowing wherein all three are present all of the time. This commitment to holistic assessment is one of the things that puts the "T" in CBTE.

Competency-based programs are built around these kinds of assessments. Key to any assessment process is clear and standardized description of the measures. This is where CBTE programs shine. The outcomes-based nature of these programs insists that learners do not pass the bar until they have shown their competence in all of the areas in which they are being measured. This is how it works. The process of assessment is the same function that achieves the desired result.

It is important to note that the learners must consent to all of this. An assessment of this depth should not be undertaken without the learner's willing participation. This is a lot to ask. While the school is learning whether the learner can be trusted, the learner is looking at the school for the exact same thing. If the learner is going to submit to this kind of scrutiny, he or she needs to know that the school can be trusted to the same degree. Will we act lovingly,

---

5   Aleshire, *Beyond Profession*, 116.

without withholding the facts the learner needs to hear?

In John 1:14, Jesus is described as bearing both "grace and truth." This is a potent combination, essential to the holistic evaluation of a learner. The learner needs to know that we will not hide the truth, but she or he also must know that we will offer it with grace. Grace does not mean that we compromise the truth. It does mean that we will express truth in the manner of the fruit of the Spirit. We will be kind and patient. We will be loving and gentle. But we will not back away from the truth. We have sometimes said to our learners that while we care deeply for them as learners, we also care for those whom they will serve in the future. For the sake of those, we need to tell the hard truths to these learners if we sometimes find that they are not measuring up to the standard that is necessary.

Truthful measurement matters. However, it is not going to be sufficient just to take the learner's measure. The degree program or educational system must also be assessed. Degree-program assessment is a hallmark concern for most accreditors. CBTE programs are particularly well suited to the task, given the fundamental way that such assessment is built into the fabric. Just as learners make progress by meeting standardized outcomes, the degree programs must be assessed against their stated program goals and objectives.

CBTE programs are not sufficient unto themselves. They are not awesome simply for the fact that they exist. These programs exist for the purpose of delivering graduates who can be trusted on mission by those in their context. The promise is that learners will not (or cannot) graduate until such proficiency has been proven. Assessment of these programs, then, will determine whether such claims can be held as true.

We cannot merely assume that the school or program is effective in its promise. Such assumptions must be measured to be ensured. We could, of course, tabulate learner achievement, but given that learners cannot achieve in a CBTE system without having proven proficiency, such quantitative assessment would almost certainly be dizzying. Some deeper means must be undertaken in order to be certain that such results are not misleading.

We would suggest both internal and external processes. Internally, we could probe learner-learning artifacts in a kind of comprehensive, randomized, and redacted system, matching the work to a standard rubric, seeking evidence that learners are achieving the levels we assume. Externally, we need to talk to the mission-holding agencies that we serve, seeking evidence that we are achieving the results that they are trusting us for.

Graduate placement rates might be one means of assessing quality. But such evaluation ought to be longitudinal as well. Can we affirm that these learners are still flourishing over time? The nature of CBTE programming might give us this kind of expectation. Indeed, with more than a decade of assessment data from the programs at Kairos and Northwest, we can attest to the fact that graduates continue to flourish for many years after graduation. Nonetheless, confidence in the effectiveness of CBTE programs must be affirmed by research.

Qualitative external assessment should also be pursued. We can gain such evidence by talking to the learners subsequent to their graduation but also to those they work with and even to those whom they serve. It is easy for theological schools to omit this type of self-evaluation, given the out-of-sight-out-of-mind nature of a graduate. We can easily cherry-pick prominent examples of success. These are the stories we use in our marketing brochures and websites. But what might we learn if we were to be more systematic? If we can build learner assessment systems while learners are active in our programs, we should not have a great deal of difficulty doing something similar among alumni.

We assess because we must not assume. It's actually possible for us to get things wrong—to lose our way and to forget about our focus, especially over time. Small misalignments can turn into dramatic vectors across the space of time. Taking care with assessment is about making sure we notice and correct when our course has moved off center. It is not hard to guard against deliberate malfeasance. It is harder to notice mistaken or nondeliberate malfunction. Diligent assessment processes protect the assurance of our promise. It helps make sure that we stay on mission.

As mentioned above, we believe that learner assessment ought to be longitudinal if it is to be holistic. Another way we can approach this is to do significant front-end assessment, strongly correlated to the outcomes of the program. If, for example, the goal of a program is to develop people for pastoral ministry, then we believe there should be effort made to ensure that learners are assessed for their capacity and call early in the program. In some programs, this may happen before the learners even enter the program.

CBTE programs require a large amount of investment on behalf of mentors and their contexts. In some cases, the financial investment by donors might be significant. We believe that we should invest our energies in proving the potential learner's gifts and sense of call before we all agree to engage in such a significant journey.

Of course, our accreditors will demand this of us. As assessment is the fundamental nature of a CBTE program, accreditors should be expected to examine closely whether the school's system is adequate for the task. This will require some precision in determining whether the program has been sufficient to deliver on the school's articulated outcomes. This is one of the advantages of CBTE programming. When built correctly, these programs are rich in data, offering the necessary information to ensure quality for the learners and churches that we serve.

It is common for learners to self-select for ministry and for programs that claim to prepare them for specific work. Anyone who has spent significant time around seminaries will know that just because learners think they are called does not mean that they are going to flourish in the pursuit of ministry. We have found it to be important to talk to the learner's church and personal network to see whether there are other credible people who could bear witness to a learner's gifts and call. We especially think it is important to talk to the learner's spouse, as this journey will demand a lot of the entire family. A process that invites discernment of this nature will not guarantee learner success. We might even get things wrong, at times, but we will be far more efficient in our investments if we count the cost before we start.

Kent recalls a learner who came to Northwest seeking enrollment in a CBTE program. In fact, it was the learner's church that brought this person to our attention. The school liked the learner a lot. His gifts were immediately evident, but there were also aspects of concern, particularly in relation to his marriage. Through an extensive and collaborative discernment process that included the learner, his spouse, his church, and professional counselors, Northwest determined not to grant admission. Instead, it encouraged the learner to engage in a period of reflective, professional marital counseling and to process what was learned in dialogue with his mentors at the church. The learner was clearly disappointed, but he heard what was said and followed the advice. Two years later, the church once again referred him to the program. The difference was remarkable. The growth in this learner exceeded the marked improvement in his marriage. He was invited to participate in the program and has flourished. We can only imagine what might have been lost if we had prematurely allowed admission.

We have many such stories, but it is important to note that this kind of front-end discernment must never be managed by the school alone. It is important to keep the church or ministry context fully and equally involved. The school will never be properly positioned to make such assessments on its own. But of course, that is how CBTE programs are built. We are simply asking that we engage with the vocational context of the learner from first contact.

Prior learning assessment is also part of the front-end process. While the comparison of work done at alternate schools can be like assessing apples for their orange-ness, CBTE programming allows us to assess a broader range of prior learning. We love to allow learners to advance more quickly in areas where their proficiency is already shown. Our only caveat is that we have a chance to see it for ourselves. Transcripts from elsewhere do not cut much ice in a CBTE context. Assessment, however, allows us to see these things in action. The structure of our programs allows us the means to affirm those things that are already in evidence.

Front-end assessment is only the start, of course. We have also learned that, in a comprehensive program like an MDiv, it can be important to build some kind of early, midrange assessment. Consider building in a checkpoint at the one-year anniversary of a learner's intake. We have found that this is a good moment for everyone to ask themselves whether things are working. Perhaps a midcourse correction would be warranted.

Might there need to be a shift in the learner's context? Are there any issues on the learner's mentor team? Has the learner shown the necessary discipline that would instill confidence that she or he will persevere until the end? We have found it important to be willing to let a learner go if the problems are persistent. Throwing good investment after bad is not helpful to anyone, especially not to the learner. We have had churches thank us for being willing to do the hard thing. The good news is that our record is almost spotless for those who clear this hurdle. If learners can make it for a year, they can make it to the end.

There are financial implications, of course. Committing to front-end assessment will be difficult if we are depending upon these learners for survival. This is why healthy financial stewardship is important. We cannot afford to be in a position where our financial well-being is dependent upon our ability to recruit learners. Subsequent chapters will describe how to finance a CBTE program so that this kind of selectivity is possible. This is a good thing not only for the financial health of the school and program, but also so that we can afford to choose our learners carefully. We have to be able to say no to people who are not ready. To do otherwise not only is poor stewardship but approaches malpractice.

Graduation is, of course, the crowning assessment. In many of our programs we have built a kind of capstone experience, where the learner is encouraged to display a cumulative and summative expression of proficiency. These are incredible moments, as learners, mentors, and people from the ministry context and mission-holding agency come together to affirm and celebrate the graduate's achievement. This is harvest time and can be absolutely beautiful.

Submitting to assessment can be painful, especially when it is holistic. Few employees relish the opportunity for annual review. It's tough to gear up emotionally for this kind of confrontational event, no matter how kind the evaluator intends to be. People are fragile, and it is difficult for us to process even the most constructive criticism. It takes a significant amount of mental health to be able to take critique in the best-intended manner, let alone in less productive and appreciative environments.

It also takes a lot of trust. CBTE programs rely on trust. It is risky. The risk learners take in trusting us to mentor them well and graciously should not be understated. But that very act of trusting is part of what allows learners to become the people they aspire to be. When the school is humble enough to build an educational system that does not revolve around itself and the interests of its own branding, they might just be worthy of a learner's confidence. Only when this trust is proven as real will our assessments show the things that we desire. Only then can our promise be proven to be true.

Competency-based systems have an advantage in that this kind of appreciative and gracious assessment is the entire substance of the process, from beginning to end. Programs that are developed around holistic assessment build stronger, more assured graduates who will have cultivated a lifetime pattern of self-critique and appreciative inquiry. Everything gets better through productive measurement. People who have demonstrated proficiency in this way of being will be people we can trust to lead us well.

CHAPTER 3

THE PRACTICES OF COMPETENCY-BASED THEOLOGICAL EDUCATION

Along with the six principles of CBTE, there are six organizational practices that create fertile soil for CBTE. Taken together, these principles and practices are intended to create a platform on which a vast array of discipleship journeys can be built. From stewarding followers of Jesus who flourish as pastors or parachurch leaders to stewarding those who thrive as software engineers, real estate agents, and financial planners, CBTE programs have the potential to create fresh expressions of education that move us toward integrative living as citizens of the kingdom. The six practices are (1) affordable programs, (2) unified systems, (3) flexible technology, (4) collaborative governance, (5) continuous improvement, and (6) quality framework.

AFFORDABLE PROGRAMS

When we talk about affordability, we tend to speak in terms of what a learner pays. To address affordability issues, then, we raise funds to provide scholarships. But every president knows this doesn't really address the affordability of the education but only the cost to learners. Providing scholarships simply shifts the burden of cost to other parts of the church. Since CBTE, at its core, is collaborative participation in the Great Commission, we must create programs that are inherently less expensive to operate and that encourage more faithful stewardship of the resources God provides.

Stewardship is an important aspect of strategic thinking, but if we don't hold strategy in tension with stewardship, we run the risk of developing systems of theological education driven by money rather than mission. In the article "Sustainability and Strategic Thinking in Theological Education," Chris Meinzer, who has more than twenty years of experience working with seminary data and currently serves as senior director of administration for the Association of Theological Schools, wrote, "I believe the largest driver in how schools utilize their human, financial, and physical resources is . . . history."[1]

If our financial stewardship runs consistently with our history, it is important for us to acknowledge that our history has been formed in the siloed approach to education that has defined modern higher education. The result is that we have created a system in which we tend to justify charging fees that burden learners with unsustainable debt and/or the church with unnecessary cost. While some schools have done great work to combat this challenge, primarily through the daunting task of raising money for financial aid, the fact is that much of that work still allows history to be the driving force behind

---

1   Chris A. Meinzer, "Sustainability and Strategic Thinking in Theological Education," *In Trust Magazine*, Autumn 2019, https://intrust.org/Magazine/Issues/Autumn-2019/ Sustainability-and-strategic-thinking-in-theological-education.

decisions. The "cost" of theological education continues to rise at an alarming rate—and learners are shouldering the burden.

It doesn't have to be this way. CBTE invites us to look for new solutions rather than try to secure funds for what we have always done. We must shift from asking, How can we fund quality education? to, How can finance be understood as part of the learning ecosystem which follows the rhythms of the learning journey in a way that allows all stakeholders to flourish? There is no rule that says high-quality theological education must be expensive. In fact, we might suggest that tuition and quality are inversely correlated. The wider the chasm between the church and the academy, the higher the sticker price of tuition will most likely be.

How Did We Get Here?

As modern higher education took its shape over the past few centuries, it was deeply formed in a context where content was assumed to be scarce—and in many ways it was. As a result, systems and structures were developed to make the production and sale of content more efficient—structures that tended to value silos over integration. The approach was helpful when access to the world's information was managed by a few particular people and places. Unfortunately, this also accelerated the professionalization of theological education and the "transformation of the commons of shared intergenerational wisdom into private property."[2] From a financial perspective, this approach also turned content delivery into a fixed cost (something schools already had plenty of). Over time, fixed-cost and content-driven classrooms became the driving force behind the learner's development. The tuition model to support this approach was built around credit hours, which became the means by which these content-driven classrooms were quantified (even though that was not the original intention). Schools leveraged these courses to provide what they felt the church needed. The goal

---

2   Ted A. Smith, *The End of Theological Education* (Grand Rapids: William B. Eerdmans, 2023), 144.

became demonstrating cognitive understanding of a certain "body of knowledge." At the time, this approach made logical sense and seemed to be the most affordable and efficient way to develop educational models. Today, all that has changed.

Information is no longer housed in institutions but is widely available. There is always more content than anyone (faculty, experts, etc.) or any institution (universities, libraries, journals, databases, etc.) can keep up with. There will always be more and more content, which means more and more specialization. It also means that the economic value of content is constantly declining. If we understand our primary role to be content providers, we have both an educational and financial problem. Conversely, when we embrace the fact that knowing is integrative and that relationships are the most transformational means by which learners can be developed for their vocations, we can begin to see a new way forward.

What Next?

Competency-based theological education provides an opportunity to imagine systems of theological education that are genuinely affordable, meaning that they do not require chasing funds to manage fixed costs or developing learning pathways that are only viable if bunches of learners participate. CBTE upends the conventional financial paradigm with an affordable system that leverages (1) variable costs, (2) new tuition models, and (3) the vast resources available outside of the academy.

Variable costs. Costs become variable instead of fixed because mentor relationships are the driving force behind the learner's development, not the classroom. While a learner may participate in wonderful and important classroom experiences, those experiences are neither what the learner is measured by nor the primary mechanism that propels the learner forward, meaning that we can utilize such methods more judiciously. This one reality can dramatically lower an institution's fixed costs. Rather than building an educational pathway around "providing content," CBTE invites the learner, with the guidance and support of a mentor team, to acquire, integrate, and display learning—that is, to develop holistic knowledge. The expenses of a school, therefore, rise and fall in sync with learning rather than with the value and production of content.

Obviously, all of this requires a new vision for the role of faculty, staff, and administrators. In our experience, those who embrace a CBTE approach to learning and the operational practices to support it find freedom in their new role. Perhaps most exciting is that the variable nature of the revenue and costs allow people to decide where and how to invest their energies. While CBTE does require us to revisit topics that were once sacrosanct, we have found those conversations to be life-giving.

New tuition models. With learning, rather than content delivery, being the center of the educational journey, it makes less sense to build tuition models around things like credit hours. Most schools doing CBTE have found that subscription pricing is a better option. By using a low-price, recurring tuition model, learners no longer need to worry about what they are going to pay for a particular semester, and institutions do not need to build budgets around unknown revenue streams. This gives both parties cost certainty.

For the school, subscription payments mean that there is no need to worry about how something like drop/add week impacts a learner's tuition. Financial aid processes do not need to include meticulous tracking of learner enrollment.

For the learner, subscription payments mean that they have clarity and control over their tuition payments. They know exactly what it is going to cost because there are no additional fees, no changes based on financial aid, and no adjustments due to course enrollment or progress. They also can control the pace of their progress and stop at any time.

Wider view of resources. Perhaps the most exciting aspect of CBTE is the way it honors the vast resources outside of the academy. It invites us to lean into the fact that seminaries do not hold all of the knowledge necessary for developing learners. When we embrace that reality, we learn that our partners are empowered to walk alongside us in more substantial ways. In many ways, they can provide learning experiences that would be impossible for us to replicate. Instead of asking, What do we need to add to our content? we can ask, Which partners are already doing good work? That question opens our eyes to the fact that the educational journey is not about us. It is about the learner and the learner's context. With that new lens, we realize how much learning, content acquisition, and development of proficiency happens outside the walls of our schools and beyond what the faculty at a school can provide. That reality spreads the power and privilege of the educational journey throughout the entire body of Christ, which ultimately reduces the price of tuition and the cost to educate learners.

In short, when taken as a whole, CBTE creates a system of theological education that is truly affordable because it stewards the abundant resources God has provided and asks the question, How can finances be understood as part of the learning ecosystem, following the rhythms of the learning journey in a way that allows all stakeholders to flourish?

UNIFIED SYSTEMS

As we have been developing CBTE programs over the past ten-plus years, a significant number of organizations, denominations, schools, and others across the landscape of theological education have asked us questions about the various principles of CBTE (e.g., customized proficiency, team-based mentoring). Very few have asked about organizational practices. In our experience, that is because of a tendency to shy away from the most pressing issue within theological education—"disintegration."

We contend that the vast majority of the challenges within theological education are symptoms of this more systemic, deep-seated issue. That is to say, the structures, systems, and ways of being that have been shaped and formed by centuries of modern higher education tend to be segmented, siloed, and departmentalized.

As an organizational practice that requires us to let go of not only power but also our perceptions of clarity, unified systems invite schools to consider how our modern systems, structures, departments, and policies have a deformational or negative impact on learning and discipleship.

Think about it: no matter how automated or integrated we try to make things, the reality is that the bedrock of conventional education was formed by a commitment to siloed disciplines, separate departments, shared (rather than collaborative) governance, and segmented operational practices. Arguments have been made suggesting that theological education's propensity to be prohibitively expensive, inaccessible, and often perceived as irrelevant stem from organizational structures and educational philosophies that encourage independence, competitive mindsets, and power struggles.

It is important to point out that, over this same period of time, there have been benefits of and changes to the way we have been doing things. Obviously, great work has been done by seminaries to address these challenges, and much can be learned from those attempts. At the same time, however, our experience has shown that CBTE unlocks the potential for high levels of integration in ways that conventional education will struggle to reproduce.

To start, we must recognize that each aspect of an educational system is dependent upon and impacted by every other aspect. Nothing happens in a vacuum. Therefore, decisions cannot be made without thinking about the entire system. CBTE more fully embraces this reality. To function well as an educational philosophy, CBTE invites us to remove departmental lines, distribute innovation, and integrate disciplines.

Remove Departmental Lines

Creating an organization that embraces the concept of integration is no simple task because it invites us to blur departmental lines that have shaped our way of being as seminaries since the mid-1800s. Departments, functional areas, and governance categories have defined how we go about our work—often more so than the discipleship task at hand. In short, our work is designed as it is, at least in part, because of the segmented structures of our organizations.

Here again, CBTE opens doors to new ways of thinking, or at least creates space for deep examination of our departmental way of being. A learner engaged in a CBTE program will, by necessity, have fluid interaction with several different aspects of a seminary. She may work with faculty, mentors, administrators, alumni, financial supporters, board members, and other learners for a single project or assignment. Staff members may find themselves in conversations about program design, and faculty may end up in conversations about financial operations.

For this reason, at Kairos we refrain from restricting meeting attendance based on title or role. Meetings, even board meetings, are open to anyone, and all who come are invited to fully participate in the conversation. The key is to move away from meetings defined by role or title and toward meetings and conversations that include everyone and take account of the entire enterprise.

Because CBTE fosters conversations, interactions, and educational modalities that intentionally stretch across disciplinary and departmental lines, it challenges long-held assumptions about the value of such departments and disciplines. It is not that the specific types of study associated with a particular discipline or the tasks that are connected to certain departments are no longer valuable. It is that CBTE calls attention to the fact that their value is best stewarded when that study and those tasks are part of an integrated whole. Rather than working to create even more definition to our disciplines or departments, we should be looking for ways to remove such boundaries.

Departmental lines tend to create power struggles, divisive policies, and systems of engagement that are not learner-centered. Removing them simply means developing an organizational culture or way of being that sees the entire educational enterprise as one integrative system. It is this approach that connects the powerful educational philosophy of CBTE to the revolutionary paradigm shift that it can be.

For example, learners in a CBTE community are part of a mutual learning environment—one in which the learner, her mentors, and her vocational context are working, learning, and developing together. As a result, relationships, trust, hard conversations, and emotional investment become hallmarks of one's participation in a CBTE program. It should not be surprising to learn, therefore, that these relationships begin to cross conventional boundaries within institutional life.

The fact is that CBTE requires us to recognize the importance of cohesive and integrated approaches to relationship development. The program itself becomes the mechanism by which we can build, cultivate, and steward relationships. If done correctly, we will see that fundraising, relationship development, marketing, operations, financial structures, program design, teaching, communication, and so on flow seamlessly throughout the CBTE paradigm. To do this effectively, we must be formed in a new way of being—one that sees us thinking more broadly about our roles and our relationship to the comprehensive work of the school.

This doesn't mean that development officers become professors and professors become enrollment managers. It does, however, mean that development officers may be better able to do their work if they serve on a few mentor teams, and that faculty may be better mentors if they spend time engaged in conversations about how mentor teams impact enrollment management.

As we practice this blurring of departmental (even organizational) lines, we begin to create tangible expressions of the new power dynamics present within CBTE. If we remove departmental lines we are, by definition, raising voices that have not traditionally been welcome at the table. Perhaps where this is most visible is in the task of innovation.

Distribute Innovation

Innovation in theological education has been an interesting thing to watch over the past number of years. While much time and energy has been put toward the development of new educational models, this work still suffers from the disintegration described earlier. As a result, the conversations or actions related to innovation tend to be limited to a particular group or department within a school. Even in cases where schools have developed task forces related to innovation, which may include people from various departments, contexts, and roles within a school (e.g., faculty, admins, board, learners), these teams still function under the auspices of a particular department or segment of the governance structure. In practice, this means that, even with an "integrated" team of people, the real choices or decisions around innovation often rest in the hands of "disintegrated" structures. As a result effective innovation, or innovation that has the potential to bring lasting change, rarely occurs.

As schools embrace CBTE, more and more people within the organizations begin to have access to more information. What was once hidden in a classroom, or in unreadable or inaccessible assessment reports, is now on display for mentors, staff, and ministry partners to experience in real time. Because of the fluid interaction with several aspects of the institution, people who were once not part of conversations about innovation may now have more information than those who once governed the innovation process.

The simple point is that CBTE, through the practice of unified systems, invites—perhaps requires—innovation to originate from anywhere within an organization. This is a good thing but is, perhaps, the most recognizable shift in power, which means it is often easier said than done.

Because CBTE does not conform to semesters, credit hours, departments, or modalities and distributes information throughout an organization, we should expect the power of innovation to be distributed across the organization as well. It means fully embracing the fact that, for example, a staff member might be the one to develop an innovative approach to learning, while a faculty member might create new opportunities related to finance. A board member might have an innovation connected to daily operations, and an office manager may provide insight related to board governance.

Integrate Disciplines

The last aspect of unified systems comes through the fact that CBTE invites us to take advantage of the reality that learning is nonlinear. It encourages proficiency of integration, not simply disciplines. To fully embrace the cross-disciplinary nature of theological education, the organization's processes and practices need to be unified and become mutually reinforcing.

As learners progress through their journey of discipleship, they are empowered to leverage moments in time that naturally encourage integrated learning. As one would expect, when we engage in, respond to, and reflect on real-life situations, we discover that life is not neatly divided into discrete disciplines. In the crucible of life, we find that proclaiming the gospel is as much about biblical study as it is about leadership, and that leadership is as much about formation as it is about strategy.

Unified systems support this type of learning because they help us remove boundaries that once reinforced discipline-specific activities. In conventional approaches to education, we tend to have the "biblical studies department" be responsible for certain aspects of learning, while the "theology department" paid attention to others. "Program directors" did the work of administering learning activities, while the "business office" thought about how to manage access through pricing. The "dean's office" would then be responsible for trying to bring all of it together. As a result, things like developing programs, building budgets, hiring faculty, envisioning course schedules, and assessing student learning tended to happen with specific disciplines or departments in mind. In a CBTE approach, opportunities for guided learning need to be available when and how learners need or desire to access them. The "just-in-time" learning that occurs within CBTE pushes against our historic tendency to segment not only learning activities by discipline (i.e., through discrete courses) but also organizational activities like meetings, communication, strategic planning, and budgeting.

That type of segmentation unintentionally creates friction in learners' educational journeys because they bump into lines of demarcation that make it difficult to leverage those real-life, inte-grated moments in time that are key to learning, growth, and for-mation. In those moments, learners and mentors need the freedom to access and engage with any collection of disciplines, learning activities, and personnel that will be most helpful in that moment. The practice of unified systems removes this friction and thereby supports CBTE in extraordinary ways.

FLEXIBLE TECHNOLOGY

When it comes to theological education, schools are notori-ously slow to adopt new technology. When we do, it tends to be technology designed for institutions rather than humans. As such, the technology we use often reinforces the operational, educational, and financial practices that have come to define higher education. As with the organizational practices of affordable programs and unified systems, the practice of flexible technology invites us to move past institutional thinking toward networked, collaborative thinking that fosters integration and customized learning.

Here's the problem: the technological systems that support most of higher education, no matter how integrated they claim to be, still tend to assume that each aspect of the institution is a wholly separate function. As a result, the software is often designed not around humans but around the departments of a school.

For example, learning management systems (LMS) are often designed to integrate with student information systems (SIS), which assume that learners enroll in particular terms and pay a particular amount per credit hour. The automation that comes from such inte-gration means that student information from an SIS is shared with an LMS. For example, when a student is enrolled in a course in the SIS, she is also given access to that course in the LMS. To aid in this "auto-mation" or "integration" of systems, companies have sought to develop software packages that offer everything—a learning management module, a student information system module, a financial services module, a fundraising module, and so on. The goal in this approach is that schools will purchase an entire system from a single provider.

It's not that these systems are bad. In fact, some of them have helpful features that do, in fact, aid in the institutional management of learners. The issue is that they unintentionally reify educational structures that end up having undue power and influence on student learning. Their goal is to streamline institutional workload and, to do that, they make assumptions about what learning is, how it is structured, and how access is managed. The driving force, therefore, is the institution rather than the student or learning. For example, student registration processes are often driven by credit hours, semesters, registration timelines, and the like—all of which assume learning happens in discrete blocks that can be stacked together. We tend to price these by the credit hour, which ends up determining how we approach budgeting, institutional planning, staffing, and more. As a result, our institutional structures drive the learning process. Our practices shape and form the institution, but they also have a formational impact on learners in that they shape how learners envision and approach learning (i.e., learning is segmented, time-based, and driven by content).

CBTE invites us to become more aware of what it means to be learner-centered and, thereby, more aware of how our systems, structures, and processes have tended to be focused on the institution. As a customizable journey of discipleship, CBTE requires technological systems that (1) encourage customization and consistency, (2) are built using a mobile-first stack of solutions, and (3) are designed around the learner (human-centered) rather than courses or institutions. Also, (4) they need to be priced differently. Let's take a brief look at those aspects.

Customization and Consistency

In our conversations with people who are exploring CBTE for the first time, we have noticed that two common assumptions are often made. People either assume that (1) it is just a new kind of distance learning wherein learners sit in front of a screen to complete online courses, or (2) learners never use traditional learning experiences like seminars, courses, or intensives. While our experience is not exhaustive by any means, learners in all of the CBTE programs of which we are aware participate in myriad learning experiences ranging from self paced, asynchronous, and project-based learning to seminars, intensives, and traditional semester-long courses. Learning may take place on the campus of a school with portions online and other bits at a church, nonprofit, or local business. CBTE encourages—we might say requires—participation in a wide range of learning experiences. As a result, the software used to support CBTE programs must be designed to handle everything from synchronous online events to on-campus residencies to asynchronous endeavors, all while tracking progress toward customized proficiency and involving mentor teams. That means the technology needs to allow extensive customization and to support consistency.

Many believe this paradox of customization and consistency creates a technological challenge because the technology to encourage customization is often assumed to be much different than the technology required to support consistency. But it doesn't have to be that way. When software puts the learner (i.e., human) first, we will find it is possible to do both at the same time.

Embracing flexible technology may be difficult at first—administrators may find it cumbersome. That feeling often stems from the belief that quality is best governed by segmenting learning into disciplines, unifying definitions of proficiency, controlling the path a learner takes, and departmentalizing organizational functions—all of which lead to technological solutions that are designed to simplify how control is enforced. Just as CBTE requires a paradigm shift in educational philosophy, it also requires a shift in technology.

Mobile-First Stack of Solutions

One way to lean into the idea of flexible technology is to begin thinking about a mobile-first stack of solutions. Doing so will make us more responsive and open to ongoing and unending change. In the past, schools hunted for single pieces of software that would handle "everything" we do as an institution. Often, these pieces of software assumed that people would be using them while sitting at a desktop computer or a full-size laptop. These assumptions resulted in high costs (such systems were exorbitantly expensive and often sold as capital investments), high commitment (such systems required multiyear commitments, often trading reduced costs over time for locked-in contracts), and experiences that varied based on the type of the device being used (which increases costs related to IT support).

The promise of these legacy systems was that everything in the institution would be integrated. In practice, however, the systems didn't fit with the day-to-day realities of serving learners well. As a result, staff created "shadow systems" to achieve basic tasks, thereby eliminating the hoped-for integration. In fact, Greg was once a culprit of such work! He built an entire automated financial aid system using Excel rather than the module embedded in the software purchased by the institution.

A better way forward is to embrace a *mobile-first* and *stack* approach to software. The mobile-first part of that statement means working with software that is designed first to work on a mobile device (smaller screens) and then to work on a laptop or desktop computer. Today's reality is that learners, mentors, faculty, and administrators are engaging in work and the learning process using mobile devices more than any other type of device. In short, if the software doesn't work seamlessly on a mobile device (smartphone, tablet, etc.), it doesn't work.

The "stack" portion of the statement invites us to stop searching for and investing in one piece of software that attempts to do everything. Instead, we build a stack of software solutions in which each part of the ecosystem does one thing very well. In this approach, a school looks for simple and task-specific solutions that leverage modern data architecture with things like REST APIs, options for leveraging online automation tools, triggers and actions, and ready-built integration with other platforms, each of which will be introduced in chapter 4. The root idea is that each piece of software can focus on a specific purpose, which means that the institution can switch out pieces of the stack as necessary rather than hitching the wagon, so to speak, to an expensive legacy system. A stack approach does mean that staff and faculty will need to have a different (and often growing) relationship with technology. Rather than seeking to be experts with a particular technological system, we must develop the ability to adapt to and leverage an array of technology that will change over time. Being learner-centered means recognizing that technology is not stationary. This nonstationary reality fosters a human-centered approach.

Human-Centered Systems
    Lastly, we need software that is human-centered rather than institution-centered. By this statement, we are attempting to call attention to the fact that software designed for educational institutions tends to be developed around the assumption that the institution is at the center of the learning experience, or at least the most important part of the equation. As a result, the software tends to reinforce long-held assumptions about how education should work, thereby placing institutional concerns (and the disintegration referenced above) at the center of the equation.
    Given the fact that CBTE challenges this institution-centric approach to education, we should not be surprised that a paradigm shift in technology will invite us to think differently about everything from learning-experience design and engagement to learner assessment and support. We contend that human-centered software, which places the learner's needs above institutional needs, will require institutions to make wholesale changes to everything from their financial models to registration processes and credit hours to collecting learning artifacts—and this is a good, even necessary, thing!
    Human-centered technology that supports CBTE is built around how people learn in real life rather than simply digitizing content and "delivering" it to learners. CBTE is not about delivering something; it is about walking with someone. It will allow mentors, learners, faculty, and administrators to develop learning

pathways that meet people where they are and help them get to where they need to be in light of their call, context, and community. Software that is human-centered empowers mentors and faculty to adjust developmental pathways in real time as opportunities for integrated learning become available, rather than be trapped inside static pathways.

Flexible Pricing

If a seminary within the Association of Theological Schools is looking at new software for CBTE (or simply software for any task), one of the best indicators of flexibility is pricing. If the software requires a multiyear contract or the sales approach invites the organization to commit to a multiyear agreement, our suggestion is to run away. While it is not always the case, often such systems fail to be flexible. In the software world, they are commonly referred to as "legacy" systems. The founder of a large software company once put it this way in a conversation with Greg: "God was able to create the universe in six days because he wasn't dealing with a legacy system."

Multiyear or long-term contract pricing tends to push against the flexibility and variable-cost financial models that often help CBTE initiatives thrive. A mobile-first stack of software that is based on some sort of variable and/or subscription pricing model creates the opportunity for the school to learn with the learners. As we work with learners, mentors, faculty, and partners, we will no doubt discover ways in which we can improve our work. Making those changes is a lot easier when our programs are not tied up in legacy pricing models.

How all of this works will vary based on practice and context. The key, however, is that we put humans at the center of the design process rather than searching for software that enables us to "automate" or "integrate" conventional approaches to education. As an organizational practice, flexible technology requires us to recognize that education is about humans interacting with other humans in real time.

COLLABORATIVE GOVERNANCE

Children are taught to share—toys, time with loved ones, and turns on things like swings and playground equipment. Learning to share is often a difficult process because we struggle to fully understand the concept. Take, for example, an experience Greg had with his two little girls, who were four and two at the time. The four-year-old received a pen for Christmas. It was a fun little pen that could change colors if you pressed the right buttons, and the mechanical features of it added a little intrigue beyond the normal pens she used when doodling at home.

A few months later, she was drawing with the pen, and the younger sister asked if she could use it. In prototypical fashion, the older one responded quickly with "No! It's mine!" Greg responded in the moment like most parents would. He asked the four-year-old to share her pen. She did, and the two-year-old began to color delightfully on the paper in front of her. All was good with the world until the next day.

The following day, the four-year-old was again drawing with her pen, and the younger one came to ask if she could use it. Having "learned" to share the pen the day before, the older one politely said, "Sure! You can use it." Greg was pleased with the interaction, and the four-year-old was so happy to know she had shared. This time, however, the two-year-old chose to use the pen as a percussion instrument! Rather than coloring nicely on the paper in front of her, she began pounding out some beats on the table!

Obviously, this mortified the four-year-old, who abruptly reached over, forcibly removed the pen from her sister's hand, and shouted, "No! You can't do that with it. It's mine!" It seemed the four-year-old was perfectly fine with sharing as long as the two-year-old did exactly what the four-year-old thought she should be doing with it.

We suggest that this is exactly how shared governance often works in seminaries. The concept of shared governance is ingrained in the structures and accreditation standards that shape higher education. Unfortunately, the way we have approached it has fostered power struggles, infighting, turf wars, institutional silos, and disconnection from those we claim to serve. It seems that, in most instances, shared governance is structured around the idea that the work of the institution is divided among the board, faculty, and administration. This is how we "share" the institution's governance. The problem, however, is that by structuring it in this way we create a situation wherein true collaboration is nearly impossible. Over time, the lines between the three areas get more clearly defined, and the space between the groups grows each year.

While we talk about how the work of the institution (e.g., assessment, strategic planning, program development) must include voices from each group, the reality is that we often fight over who has "ultimate" power or control. This kind of collaboration devolves into something like the conversation between Greg's little girls. The administration may "share" strategic planning with the faculty until the faculty decides to use it in a way that the administration believes wasn't intended, at which point the administration says, "No! You can't do that with it. It's mine!" The faculty may share program development with the board and administration until they see it isn't being used "correctly," at which point they also say, "No! You can't do that with it. It's mine!" Perhaps the worst part is the fact that our common approach to shared governance completely emaciates voices outside the walls of the institution. By fighting with each other over power, control, or strategy, we lose the opportunity to fully engage those we claim to serve.

CBTE offers, perhaps requires, a fresh expression of governance. It invites us to think of governance not as something we divide and conquer (share), but as something we steward collaboratively. As a collective body of Christ-followers who have been entrusted with resources and a mission, we should engage in a trust-based collaborative approach to governance. In this approach, power and prestige are released by every person and group within an institution in order to welcome everyone to the table. Systems and structures need to be as flat as possible, allowing all voices to speak with power into the work of an institution.

In doing so, we will not only give away internal power but also welcome the church as our primary collaborator. When we begin to trust each other and see governance as a collaborative process, we are more able to let go, not only of individual power but also of institutional power. This release of power opens doors to conversations that are currently closed and empowers the church to be fully invested in the development of disciples, which is a key aspect of CBTE.

In this way, collaborative governance can be disruptive in that it upends a more traditional model of organizational development—one in which only certain voices are most often heard. This elevation of concerns and voices that often are not heard can be perceived as a diminishing of the concerns and voices of those most often heard in conventional systems. This can be unsettling at the beginning of the change process. It is also disruptive because, once the trust-based collaborative culture and governance structure has been created, the conventional processes for including voices become antiquated and harmful. New processes for including voices must be developed, and these new processes will, in turn, liberate the institution from the bondage of silo-thinking.

CBTE requires us to recognize that wisdom exists outside of the academy, that best practices for education can be developed by people who are not faculty members, and that business operations and strategy can be highly informed by people other than CEOs, CFOs, and board members. In short, the community of faith that is invested in the mission of a school is best served when that community stops worrying about who has the power and control and instead focuses on its common mission. Collaborative governance is only possible when we have a shared mission and shared values. That is where the challenge actually resides.

The community must be reminded of the institution's espoused values, mission, and strategic direction. Many of us have not done the hard work of aligning our espoused values and mission with our daily practices as an organization. We struggle with collaboration because the silos are not actually trying to accomplish the same things. In order to be collaborative, we must move past thinking that collaboration is simply "including voices" or "making sure everyone is heard." Instead, we must align our mission with those we serve by giving away power once reserved for particular voices of our institutions. In that process, we will begin to see how our practices do not align with our espoused values.

We contend that CBTE fosters this type of conversation in a way that conventional models of education never will because it sheds light on every aspect of the institution's actions. It calls attention to how we plan and who is engaged in that work. It highlights the ways in which our financial planning is controlled by things that are disconnected from learning and discipleship. It creates pathways for new voices to bring new insights because every learner brings with her a mentor team, perhaps a partner organization, and new vocational complexities. Because the underlying assumption of CBTE is that significant learning happens outside of the artificial realities we create and control as institutions, it tends to reveal areas in which our espoused values and organizational practices are misaligned. This misalignment is magnified because a wider community is now engaged in the process of developing leaders. To make the needed adjustments, we must implement governmental structures that distribute power and raise voices that were once on the sidelines.

In one example, a partner organization called attention to the way in which a school's theological statements on its website did not align with its espoused value of global engagement. As that partner invited faculty mentors around the world to serve within the school's CBTE initiatives, those new voices were able to highlight the misalignment. The CBTE approach empowered those voices because they had a shared commitment to stewarding the mission of the school's growing global community. As a result, the school adjusted its statements and improved its faculty mentor-training processes.

When that happens—when we see our practices pushing against the very thing that we say is our mission—we must respond with humility and grace rather than power and prestige. The result is a collaborative-governance culture that is responsive and rooted in trust, which embraces the movement of the Spirit in the lives of those who call Jesus Lord.

CONTINUOUS IMPROVEMENT

When a CBTE program is fully operational, with learners, partners, and mentors working together in light of the principles of CBTE, the amount of assessment data flowing in and through the educational enterprise is staggering. With the blessing of new data points, schools are presented with an opportunity to think differently about how they improve learning, programs, and the institution. Rather than simply cataloging data in assessment reports that are reviewed every few years with the goal of doing macro-level program reviews, institutions engaged in CBTE are able to engage in ongoing change, thereby creating a culture of continuous improvement.

The concept of continuous improvement is not new. In our experience, the best way to learn about it is to study the product development process utilized by several contemporary software companies. We find that CBTE allows institutions to combine new opportunities for observation and evaluation with the approach to software development trumpeted by people like Jason Fried, founder and CEO of Basecamp and a leading voice in contemporary software development practices. With this approach, schools can improve programs and student learning at both the micro (individual learner) and macro (entire program and institution) levels, often closing feedback loops in real time as they respond to the data provided by the CBTE system.

In practice, this means that CBTE creates space for at least four continuous improvement accelerants: (1) ongoing change that reinforces strategy, (2) data-driven micro and macro improvements, (3) empowered feedback loops, and (4) distributed ideation.

Ongoing Change That Reinforces Strategy

When we first began the CBTE programs at our respective institutions, the strategy was to develop high-quality, competent, and wise leaders in partnership with local communities of faith. Given our higher education context, we needed to track learner progress (a data point we are required to give to accreditors, governments, denominations, etc.). Historically, that data was produced through a student information system (SIS) that tracks registration and course completion data.

After a semester or so of gathering that data, to our surprise, we noticed that the CBTE learners were making terrible progress! At the pace they were going, it was going to take ten years to finish a program—or so it seemed at the macro level. Fortunately, CBTE provided several additional data points beyond those produced by the SIS. Data from the assessments conducted by mentor teams revealed that learners were making good progress. The local churches and denominational partners were noticing an uptick in leadership capacity. In addition, data from our LMS showed that learners were indeed making progress, but that the progress was not linear. Rather than moving forward on one class or competency at a time, they were integrating their work and moving forward on several at a time. None of this data appeared in the conventional reports about learner progress

As a result, our fear about progress turned quickly to strategic conversations about messaging. We had new data and needed a way to present it to various stakeholders (e.g., board, faculty, partners, denominational leaders). As a result, we began enhancing the way our LMS presented progress to the mentor teams by disaggregating the data. We changed the way we talked about progress in our promotional, orientation, and training material. Reports for the board were adjusted to address the concepts of retention and persistence in more meaningful ways. Qualitative data points were added to our dashboards. These changes were made over the course of weeks and months rather than years. Each change was guided by the strategic direction (developing high-quality leaders) and focused on enhancing the entire CBTE system (learning, experience, assessment, reporting, etc.). The new data, mixed with a commitment to iterative change, allowed us to close the feedback loop more quickly and effectively than the conventional approach to annual assessment. CBTE inspired ongoing change that reinforced strategy. To us, that seemed to be different than what schools, even the ones we led, were doing up to that point

In our experience, it is quite common for schools to develop strategic plans and to evaluate them on an annual basis. Unfortunately, such plans often become *business* plans with "strategy" language strewn about. When this happens, the value of data is diminished by the elongated length of time between gathering the data and responding to it. Making decisions in an ongoing, iterative fashion is difficult because schools often lack the real-time data needed to make informed, data-driven decisions about potential improvements. We believe CBTE addresses this problem by inviting schools to be more direct about their strategy and to respond more immediately to relevant data.

The strategy of an organization is rooted in its mission and should be focused on a clearly articulated direction in which the organization is headed. It is focused on ends rather than means. Sure, we will discuss means, but these means to the end must be held lightly. To put it another way, our job as leaders is to discern the direction in which God is calling us. Then we create adaptable systems and structures that enable us to move in that direction and to be responsive to the terrain encountered along the way. In this approach, we expect to change and, therefore, create mechanisms for capturing and responding to data as we go.

The concept of continuous improvement assumes the ongoing development of strategic direction—that is to say strategy, rather than a business plan in and of itself, must guide the work of the institution. By focusing on a strategic direction (ends) rather than entirely on plans (means), we can hold our plans lightly, which opens the door for a continuous feedback loop!

CBTE invites us to think more strategically because it focuses on the intended ends rather than the practiced means. By embracing the fact that learning is nonlinear, we don't have to be caught up in the conventional business-plan approach to strategy. If learning is nonlinear, then our systems and processes need to be flexible. If we have flexible systems and processes, we need to have mechanisms for systematizing customization. In short, CBTE helps us to develop organizational and assessment practices that adapt to the terrain we encounter rather than assuming we know the terrain. To do this well, we need a way to see the terrain, to feel how it is moving and shifting under our feet. We need to be closer to the ground.

Fortunately, when fully invested in CBTE, we are able to see the world from a different perspective—one that is closer to the day-to-day realities of learners, partners, and local communities of faith. Because learners are using those day-to-day experiences to shape learning, we are given fresh eyes to see the ways in which micro- and/or macro-level changes in our programs and institutions might improve the entire process. These changes are driven by strategy and informed by data.

Over time, this mixture of data and ongoing change creates a culture of continuous improvement. It is a culture that hungers for change rather than fears it. The additional data points enable us to make ongoing, incremental change and larger-scale, systemic change, both of which stem from actionable data.

Data-Driven Macro and Micro Improvements

In a conventional system, a school of 150 students[3] might get input from a few points of connection: the students, the faculty who teach courses in the program's curriculum, a few engaged board members, and the staff who are connected to the assessment process. There may also be mechanisms for gathering a smattering of data from external constituencies such as employers, churches, denominations, congregational members, and staff.

Now, let's imagine the same school launching a CBTE program. Based on our experience working with several schools who

---

3   At the time of writing, data from the Association of Theological Schools showed that about 50 percent of seminaries in the United States and Canada have 150 students or fewer, so 150 is a good number to use for this example.

have launched CBTE programs, new learner enrollment tends to gravitate toward the CBTE program. In several cases, after a few years, 50 percent or more of new learners have enrolled in the CBTE program. With mentoring and collaborative structures in place, this influx of CBTE learners exponentially expands the number of connection points for a school. When the school has seventy-five learners in a CBTE program, it most likely has well over two hundred engaged mentors, sixty to seventy-five different vocational contexts, additional faculty who are serving as mentors, mission-minded partners who helped to create the program, more staff members who interact with learners along the way, an increased number of engaged board members, and a new array of learning experiences that are as unique as each of the seventy-five learners. Each one of those presents a new opportunity for data.

This is why a commitment to continuous improvement must be supported by a commitment to data-driven decisions at both the micro (individual learner) and macro (program and institution) levels. Each learner represents a network of connections to a school's system of assessment. We know more about learner progress and learning, program effectiveness, institutional vitality, mission fulfillment, and stakeholder engagement than we thought was possible. Because it is possible to be overwhelmed by the data created (or made visible) by a CBTE program, we must find a way to capture, synthesize, and respond to it.

A commitment to continuous improvement lessens the burden of this exponential increase in assessment data because it empowers institutions to make micro changes along the way to macro changes. Rather than collecting mounds of data for future use, we respond to these streams of data in real time. For example, incremental changes can be made to seminar schedules, curriculum documents, resources within an LMS, even the educational path of particular learners. These micro changes are driven by data and are made without the need for wide-ranging conversations. Over the course of a few months or a semester, data can be aggregated to suggest macro-level changes (e.g., adjustments to the user interface of an

LMS, new language within a competency or outcome statement, refreshed orientation material for new learners, curricular enhancements). With the increased presence of timely and actionable data, a school engaged in CBTE can make ongoing change that consistently improves the program. These changes are what close the feedback loop.

Empowered Feedback Loops

In our experience, well-designed and well-meaning assessment systems can come to a grinding halt when confronted with the conventional decision-making processes of higher education. The assessment data may reveal the need to adjust the curriculum, and this begins a six-month conversation on what to change. After we decide what to change, we develop a plan to implement the new curriculum, only to find that another change is needed—because the previous data is now more than a year old.

Another example could be one a friend of ours shared with us regarding the process for appointing faculty in the teaching hospital where she worked. It served as a stark reminder of the reality that well-meaning processes can push against the need for real-time action. During the COVID-19 pandemic in 2020, her teaching hospital was overwhelmed with the need for doctors. While several doctors were available, willing, able, and qualified to serve, they could not do so because each of them had to be approved as faculty in addition to being approved as doctors—a process that normally took four to six months. It is quite easy for the process of decision-making and implementation to derail any momentum that might be created by assessment data or on-the-ground feedback.

We believe that CBTE creates an opportunity to approach this challenge from a fresh perspective. With its focus on ends rather than means, CBTE invites institutions to hold lightly many things that were once sacrosanct. It is not that we completely abandon those things we once held dear. Rather, we give them appropriate weight within a system that says that outcomes, demonstrated by observable behavior and/or data, are the guides. By adjusting this weight distribution, we are able to develop faculty, staff, mentors, partners, board members, and administrators who embrace and embody this new reality, thereby empowering people to make decisions without the need for complex and cumbersome systems of oversight.

Let's take curriculum adjustments as an example. In a conventional system, conversations about curricular adjustments will no doubt be based on good assessment data and will take account of the program goals and outcomes. Eventually, however, the conversation will turn to a focus on means. We will talk about which courses, assignments, and activities learners must complete in order to address the issue noted in the data. Again, this is all well-meaning and focused on enhancing quality. After several conversations about the means, we will develop a plan for implementing the idea and a way to assess the change. The challenges with this approach are that it assumes the following: (1) the means will deliver the intended outcome, (2) each learner will respond to the means in the same way, and (3) a small group of people, who are not connected to the day-to-day life of each learner, is the right group to make this decision.

In a CBTE system, the mentor team, who is tasked with holistic and general assessment of integrated outcomes, is trained to conduct assessment in a particular way in light of program goals, rubrics, discrete competencies, and mission. As a result, when they notice that a learner is not adequately demonstrating competency, they have the power, wisdom, and competence needed to make changes in real time. They can adjust the learning pathway to account for the areas in which the learner needs more development. The team gathers data through a consistent process of assessment, reflects on the data in light of their "close-to-the-ground" knowledge of the learner and her context, works with the learner to make adjustments in real time, and closes the feedback loop by revisiting the same assessment process that surfaced the need for change. In a conventional system, we gather feedback and slowly close the loop. In CBTE, we gather feedback and close the loop in real time, all the while gathering data that can be aggregated to inform large-scale institutional/ programmatic assessment. The amount of data generated creates feedback loops that are opened and closed on a daily basis. It also creates a distributed ideation network.

Distributed Ideation

Within a culture of continuous improvement, ideas may come from anywhere, and this must be encouraged. Improvements that come from a program director, vice president, board member, office manager, learner, and partner are all valid. The source of the idea does not determine its value. If we confine ourselves to the expectations of those with the most power, we will undermine the new data provided by CBTE.

Each of those additional connection points represents a different perspective, an alternative source of feedback, and another engaged voice. The challenge is to create mechanisms for gathering that feedback, synthesizing it into actionable ideas, and responding to it. Many of the improvements we have made to the CBTE programs at our schools have come from this extended network of connections; they do not come from our full-time faculty and staff. In one case, it was a software engineer from a partner organization who suggested the layout for a learning experience library. In another instance, it was a denominational connection who suggested a different approach to clinical pastoral education within CBTE. The key is to recognize that this vast array of connections creates not only a dispersed network of learning but also a distributed system of ideation.

As a school moves more fully into CBTE, it will find that it becomes easier, even natural, to focus on continuous improvement. In our experience, it is hard to imagine any other way. We did not set out to develop a system of continuous improvement. It simply became our reality. Our message to you is to embrace that reality as you begin. Expect to make ongoing and iterative change. Expect for ideas to come from all over. You won't be disappointed.

QUALITY FRAMEWORK

Modern approaches to education tend to assume that quality is controlled through content and discipline-specific rubrics utilized in task-specific and analytic assessments conducted by experts in those particular disciplines. That assumption is often played out in curricular development practices that tend to focus on creating rigid pathways built using standardized content (i.e., syllabi), which is provided through predetermined educational experiences (i.e., courses) and facilitated (i.e., taught) by particular types of people (i.e., credentialed content experts). We refer to this as the "pyramid of courses." For many years, the academy (and the church) has tended to assume that if we take a group of learners through a predefined course of study, they will achieve particular outcomes. The thinking seems to have been, If we focus on the inputs, we will get the desired outcome.

CBTE invites us to challenge that assumption by rethinking how we understand and "control" quality. Because one's understanding of quality flows from that person's engagement in a particular community of practice, the fact is that standards of excellence (i.e., quality, proficiency, competency, etc.) cannot be universally defined. The educational philosophy of CBTE requires schools to embrace the fact that all things must be assessed with greater awareness of what proficiency looks like within a given context. To do this well, a CBTE program must have mechanisms in place that help mentor teams, learners, partners, and faculty to walk through the process of particularizing definitions of proficiency in light of a learner's context. As we step into a future of generative artificial intelligence, these mechanisms will help learners, mentor teams, faculty, partners, and schools engage thoughtfully with the unique opportunities for learning they provide.

Through CBTE, entire educational programs can be tailored to an individual learner's journey of discipleship. Rather than building a pyramid of courses, CBTE allows each learner to have a customized educational journey. To put that more simply, two learners could graduate from the same institution with the same degree and yet engage in different content, submit different assignments, and progress at different speeds. Therein lies the challenge. With that level of customization, how do we ensure quality? If quality is no longer determined by consistency of content or assignments, how is it determined?

Our answer is that while quality must be contextually defined, it can be broadly ensured through a commitment to shared language, practices, and assessment. We call this a quality framework. It empowers learners to envision a compelling path toward proficiency and allows mentors to recognize when contextualized proficiency has been achieved.

The way a quality framework is developed and applied within a particular organization will vary based on the unique context of that institution. At the same time, however, there is a growing body of work that can provide a helpful starting point.

When writing a quality framework for CBTE, it is important to remember that it is rooted in the fact that standards of excellence arise from within particular traditions and/or communities of practice. The quality framework provides a shared set of principles and practices that inform and give shape to everything we do. It reinforces the fact that quality is governed through shared processes, not shared content. Finally, a quality framework articulates how the power of program development, assessment, and engagement will be distributed throughout the learning community rather than held within a small number of internal voices.

With those key points in mind, the quality framework is written as a series of cascading interests that mutually reinforce each other. Those interests fall into five broad categories:

1. A shared understanding of how standards of excellence work
2. Principles and practices that should be present in order for a school to effectively implement and maintain a CBTE program

3. Shared design principles that must be true for all programs
4. Aspects that are particularized within each program and/or learner journey
5. Practices for training, documenting, and communicating the expectations of mentors

When developing curriculum, conventional education tends to begin with content or courses. In our experience, well-developed CBTE programs begin with clearly defined and commonly held practices and principles. These statements of belief, behavioral descriptions, and bedrock dispositions work together to form the foundation of a high-quality program. They articulate the educational philosophy, give direction to future customization, determine the way in which standards within the institution are developed, and create a shared understanding of performance indicators, inputs, rubrics, and assessment.

In our experience, institutions often underestimate the time it takes to develop a list of practices and principles that are clearly articulated, understood, and embraced across the entire institution. They are, however, the bedrock for the quality framework. A sample quality framework is included in the appendix of this book.

Finally, because quality in CBTE programs is ensured through a commitment to shared language, practices, and assessment, it is vital for an institution to have a clearly articulated process for how it will train mentors (especially faculty mentors and those in the learners' vocational contexts). This training will need to include documentation of the program and the various aspects of the quality framework. It also needs to serve as the foundation for ongoing communication between mentors and the institution. CBTE tends to foster a distributed community of learning, which means the geographic location of learners, mentors, partners, and so on may no longer be influenced by the geographic location of the institution. We think that is wonderful. With that kind of geographic distribution, we find that the processes and communication matter a great deal.

By approaching quality in this way, we not only create a more inviting and engaging learning experience but also help learners and mentors learn how to define and develop proficiency. As a result, we can ensure that learners will reach the level of proficiency that will help them flourish in their current and future vocational contexts, for the sake of the world.

CHAPTER 4

DESIGN PROPOSALS FOR COMPETENCY-BASED THEOLOGICAL EDUCATION

As we have worked with educators and agencies—seminaries, universities, nonprofits, churches, networks, and denominations—we have been privileged to facilitate hundreds of conversations on the topic of competency-based theological education. It has been a blessing to facilitate these conversations with faculty, learners, mentors, administrators, board members, and leaders of partner agencies from all around the world. At the time of writing, we have worked with people from nearly one hundred countries, spread across six different continents, and who speak an array of languages. CBTE is a global movement, and it has been exciting to see what God is doing in, through, and for those we have had the blessing to walk alongside.

MINDSET SHIFTS

These conversations have been focused on everything from program development to financial modeling, faculty/mentor training to learner experience design, and much more. Conversations about CBTE tend to invite those involved to consider a wide array of institutional practices, guiding principles, and foundational assumptions.

With the global nature of such conversations, several aspects of CBTE have been contextualized within particular cultural or vocational contexts. Mentoring, for example, might look different across cultures or vocations. Technology might be leveraged in different ways. The availability of written resources in particular languages may require adaptations in how a program thinks about and leverages inputs. We have endeavored to craft the practices and principles in light of these differences so that they can be used in conversations and program design across a wide array of cultures and contexts.

While some aspects of CBTE will (and must) be adapted in various cultures and contexts around the world, we have found that five key concepts—which we call mindset shifts—rise to the surface in each culture and context that we have encountered thus far. We are not saying that these shifts are universally applicable, since we have not worked in every culture and context. We are simply saying that, in our experience, these shifts have become important points of conversation. It seems that the areas of curriculum, excellence, control, holistic assessment, and philosophy tend to dominate the conversations.

Curriculum

Thriving CBTE programs successfully make the shift *from static content engagement to adaptive proficiency assessment.* In conventional educational programs, curriculum could be described as a system for delivering content through particular experiences and collecting artifacts from learners through particular assignments. In this kind of system, each course is often an "end" in that the purpose of the course is subsumed within the course itself. The delivery of content, therefore, becomes the driving force behind curriculum. We tend to build programs/curriculum by listing the courses someone should complete.

CBTE, on the other hand, invites us to see curriculum as a system of adaptive proficiency assessment. Courses and content are not ends. They are resources that learners can use as they wish (or do not wish). Rather than spending a lot of time carefully crafting the content and how we plan to deliver it, the curriculum development process becomes a robust, multifaceted conversation about outcomes, competencies, indicators—in other words, proficiency! Our time is spent thinking about how we observe, identify, describe, and assess proficiency. With that approach, the conventional aspects of curriculum (e.g., courses, content, modality) take their rightful place as important but secondary aspects of the curriculum. They are means, not ends. The importance of this shift cannot be overstated because of the way our entire system of education in North America has been built around the goal of generating and disseminating content. CBTE generates learners who can be trusted in the wild without close supervision. One way to encourage this shift is to embrace the idea that knowledge is the integration of content, character, and craft. That is to say that *knowing* something is more than having a cognitive awareness of it. In Scripture, to "know" Jesus is Lord or to "know" someone carries much richer meaning. The same needs to be true in our curricular endeavors. Rather than equating knowledge with content (i.e., knowing systematic theology means understanding the content of theological doctrines), we need to see knowledge as an integrative activity. When we begin to embrace the fact that knowledge is the integration of content, character, and craft, our understanding and utilization of curriculum will shift.

Excellence

When we make the shift to approaching curriculum development through the lens of adaptive proficiency assessment, we will quickly notice that it matters greatly who defines and assesses proficiency. CBTE invites us to enhance our understanding of excellence in order to appropriately assess proficiency. Conventional approaches to education place the power of defining excellence into the hands of particular faculty. While this is an important and needed voice, it cannot be the only or even the leading voice in all circumstances. We must shift *from seeing excellence as something universally defined and understood to embracing the fact that standards of excellence are contextually defined, flow from particular communities of practice, and change over time.* For example, what is deemed to be excellent leadership in one context may be detrimental in another. Effective communication varies by context, culture, and vocation. Even our understanding of what is "academic" requires contextualization.

In simple terms, this shift is one that deepens and broadens our understanding of excellence. We move from having one group of people define excellence to developing contextually appropriate processes for defining excellence that invite multiple voices into the conversation and embrace the adaptive nature of it. We tend to define "high-quality" educational journeys in terms of who is providing what type of content. Excellence, therefore, is defined by that who and what. CBTE makes visible the fact that learners are engaged in a multitude of contexts, vocations, theological traditions, and points in time. In that reality, we must shift from thinking about excellence as something that is static and universally understood to something that is dynamic and requires ongoing thoughtful reflection in order to define and demonstrate.

Control

If curriculum is more about indicators and holistic assessment, and excellence is dynamic and requires ongoing reflection, then how does control work? The short answer is that it doesn't work like it currently does in most places. In this area, the shift is *from centralized control to distributed empowerment.* In order to assess proficiency appropriately and to respond to the dynamic nature of excellence, we must empower a wider community of learning. The faculty's voice in a classroom or learning experience is one of many and often is not the closest to the day-to-day interactions of the learner. To adequately leverage the learning that takes place in those day-to-day integrations, we need to distribute the power for assessment to include mentors, peer learners, mission-holding and organizations; and distribute the control over educational pathways to include more opportunities than we can provide through institutionally controlled learning experiences.

In our experience, there is a direct correlation between complexity and trust. If the school or organization developing a CBTE program has low trust with learners, mentors, or partners, it will be a complex program and, therefore, more expensive and cumbersome to operate. Alternatively, where there is high trust, programs tend to be less complex, easier to manage, and more open to growth.

Assessment

In chapter 2, we described holistic assessment as one of the principles of CBTE. We have found it to be an essential mindset shift. In particular, we must shift *from task-specific and analytical assessment to general and holistic assessment.* While there is a place for task-specific assessment, we contend that it cannot be the driving force behind student learning, degree programs, or institutional assessment. This shift invites us to see that discerning, developing, and demonstrating proficiency is a formational endeavor that must be shaped, adjusted, and reviewed over time. Task-specific and analytical assessment tends toward a one-size-fits-all approach to student-learning assessment, which means it superimposes one definition of excellence on all learners regardless of their call, context, and tradition. That singular or uniform definition of excellence has often been driven by Western definitions of academic quality, which means we run the risk of imposing those ideals on non-Western cultures and contexts. In addition, it tends to enforce particular theological and vocational paradigms that may not fit the context of every learner—even every learner within a particular denomination or theological tradition. Holistic and general assessment brings the entire life cycle of a learner's journey through a program into view. It empowers us to take a developmental approach and feedback-oriented approach to learning, wherein what matters is the direction we are heading and the growth we are seeing as we make the journey together. In this approach, assessment becomes a tool for ongoing learning and development rather than a point-in-time measuring stick. Our tendency is to push toward ever-greater delineation of indicators so that each and every assignment or competency can be segmented into specific tasks that can be assessed. When our mindset shifts to holistic assessment, we keep the entire journey in view and provide space for partners, faculty, and the body of Christ to assess and encourage learners over time.

Philosophy

The final mindset shift we suggest is a shift *from approaching CBTE as a model or delivery method to embracing it as an educational philosophy*. Given the rise in popularity of CBTE, it is common for schools to approach it like any other program or mechanism for growing enrollment, solving financial challenges, and/or adjusting contextual models of theological education. While CBTE may help schools address such challenges and it may be necessary to refer to something as a CBTE "program," we need to refrain from envisioning it as simply another program we are launching. For it to flourish in institutions and have lasting impact on the work we do as seminaries, we need to embrace it as a paradigmatic shift in how we imagine, engage, and administer the task of stewarding followers of Jesus in the context of higher education. When we relegate it to a new program or the most recent expression of contextual education, we stunt our growth and development as a community of learners.

We have worked with schools who adopted a competency-based philosophy of theological education and yet still assess learning in the context of a traditional classroom environment, or others who imbue classic degrees (like the PhD) with competency-based principles and practices. We have also worked with schools, churches, and denominations who approached CBTE as simply a model or delivery method. In most of those circumstances, the gravitational pull toward conventional curricular structures, power dynamics, and assessment practices lead to programs that would be more appropriately defined as church-based traditional degrees. That is to say, the pace, path, and performance metrics are all governed by the school and mediated through conventional mechanisms. The only difference is that the classroom was located in a church rather than at a seminary. While we might argue that church-based programs can be a step forward, they are not a new paradigm.

To summarize, we think there are five key mindset shifts that need to take place in order for CBTE programs to thrive. We must shift from

1. thinking about curriculum as a system of static content engagement to envisioning it as a system of adaptive proficiency assessment;

2. seeing standards of excellence as something universally defined and understood to embracing the fact that they are contextually defined, flow from particular communities of practice, and change over time;

3. centralized control to distributed empowerment;

4. task-specific and analytical assessment to general and holistic assessment;

5. approaching CBTE as a model or delivery method to embracing it as an educational philosophy.

Some aspects of CBTE will (and must) be adapted in various cultures and contexts around the world, but we have found these shifts to be important topics of conversation with everyone we have engaged thus far. As you design and develop your program or organization, we urge you to include these in your discernment process.

ACCESSIBLE LEARNING

Over the past number of years, it has become trendy to talk about accessibility in education, and for good reason: we need to make it more accessible to a wider array of people. As an industry, when thinking about accessibility, we tend to focus on location (by creating online courses and programs), price (by lowering the price learners pay for a degree), time (again, by making things available online), and learning needs (creating opportunities for learners who need particular resources). All of these are good, important, and needed. We are not trying to undervalue or diminish the need for such change. When it comes to conventional education, we are putting a lot of energy toward making it more accessible.

Our question, then, is, Why does accessibility continue to be so elusive? We believe that it might be a result of the fact that conventional education constrains our approaches to accessibility. When our entire system is built around credit hours and traditional course structures, there is only so much that we can do when it comes to location, price, time, and learning needs.

CBTE, on the other hand, opens the door to new ways of thinking about accessibility. Perhaps the most important door is time. In his book *Students First: Equity, Access, and Opportunity in Higher Education*, Paul LeBlanc shed light on the importance of learner access and gave a few good examples of how time is deeply related to accessibility.

Many of us once felt that online programs would solve the issue with time. It meant that learners could participate in class at "whatever time was most convenient for them." If a learner wanted to do classwork at eleven o'clock at night, then she could. If another wanted to jump online at six, before the kids woke up, that was fine as well. Asynchronous online learning did (and still does) create the space for people to engage at the time of day that might be most helpful to them. However, because those courses are still bound by the credit hour and the conventional definitions of time associated with them (i.e., they still have to take place within a predefined period of time), learners are only able to shift time a little. They are still bound by the fact that certain assignments or activities have to be done in specific weeks or even on particular days of the week. A learner doesn't have the freedom to turn that fifteen-week theology course into five weeks or twenty-five weeks. The assignment is due on Monday, even if the kids get sick or the boss asks for some extra time on Sunday. Yes, faculty make exceptions, allow for learners to turn assignments in late, and so on. The fact remains, however, that time is still the governing factor, not learning.

CBTE, however, removes time from the equation, thereby making education more accessible. One school allows learners to begin any month of the year, while another lets them begin any day of the year. Some schools doing CBTE have specific start times, but then learners make progress at their own pace. All of this leads to greater accessibility because the learner is not beholden to the schedule and pace of the academic calendar and institution. Discretionary time is a privilege, not a given. As Paul LeBlanc pointed out in his book, a learner who has to wash his clothes at a laundromat has significantly less time than the one who has a washer and dryer at home. Conventional education requires each of those learners to complete the same amount of work in the same week but takes no account of the fact that their available time is very different. CBTE, on the other hand, welcomes this diversity of time by letting the learner set the pace, thereby making it equally accessible to the person traveling to and from the laundromat as it is for the person blessed with the privilege of doing laundry at home.

Second to time is probably money. Because conventional education is built around the financial model of selling credit hours, it privileges those who are able to purchase sums of credit hours at one time. For example, the price per credit hour at Sioux Falls Seminary before it transitioned to CBTE was $599 per credit hour. Imagine, then, the learner who plans to register for six credit hours. That will be roughly $3,600. Even if the learner makes a payment plan whereby the $3,600 is spread out over all four months of the fall semester, the learner still needs to have the financial status to plan for a bill of $3,600. Then, if we throw in scholarships, loans, discounts, or what have you, the reality is that the learner may not even know what it is going to cost. This means that education is more accessible to those with the financial means to plan for a $3,600 purchase without knowing the exact cost, all because the credit hour is the driving force behind the transaction.

With CBTE, however, we don't need to sell credit hours. Some of the schools who are thriving the most are using a subscription-based pricing model that is disconnected from credit hours. In this approach, the price a learner pays is transparent, consistent, and predictable. For some schools it is $150 per month while, for others, it is $300 or $500 per month. Keep in mind, however, that the amount is not only what makes it more accessible. Rather, predictability and transparency are key to accessibility. Income disparity will always impact accessibility in a society where education is a market-driven reality. That's an important conversation for another day. CBTE creates the opportunity for transparent and predictable pricing.

Time and money are the driving factors behind accessibility. CBTE is not the magical answer to these issues. It is, however, a new lens through which we can address both challenges. CBTE has already proven that it can make programs more accessible. The key is leveraging it to reimagine how we think about time and money.

RESOURCE AVAILABILITY

Best practice in competency-based theological education is encouraged by schools and agencies sharing resources and encouraging each other. The relative newness of the movement, especially in contrast to the centuries-old establishment of conventional forms of education, means that the availability of resources intended to support the development of CBTE programs is limited. Of course, this book is intended to help in that regard. As all of us find ways to share our experiences, we will deepen the pool of resources available to help others in their development of this approach to theological education.

The development of CBTE as a movement has benefited from the broader work of competency-based education (CBE) in general. We encourage theological educators to engage this fruitful pool of resources fully, while keeping an eye on the elements that distinguish CBTE as a theological enterprise. One of the first documents that spurred the recent development of CBE was Amy Laitinen's "Cracking the Credit Hour," published in 2012.[1] This groundbreaking report raised serious questions about the conventions of traditional education like "seat time" and the validity of the "credit hour" as the coin of the academic realm. This is an excellent place to start when trying to appreciate the impulses that have sparked this broader educational revolution.

From there, one would be well advised to engage the work of the Competency-Based Education Network, otherwise known as C-BEN. C-BEN describes itself as "a network of institutions, employers, and experts who believe competency-based learning can unlock opportunity for today's learners."[2] Its website is a treasure trove of resources for educational administrators, including quality framework documents and story-telling tool kits, as well as hundreds of other documents and presentations that can be searched for insight into most aspects of the CBE enterprise.

C-BEN serves the hundreds of universities, colleges, seminaries, and service organizations that engage the CBE world. While seminaries and theological schools will have to be discerning about their use of these materials, C-BEN as a network has been friendly to theological educators and the CBTE movement for many years. The president of C-BEN, Charla Long, was a keynote speaker at the first international CBTE conference held in Vancouver, British Columbia, in 2018. Since then, the annual C-BEN conference has

---

1   Amy Laitinen, "Cracking the Credit Hour," New America Foundation and Education Sector, September 2012, https://www.newamerica.org/education-policy/policy-papers/cracking-the-credit-hour.
2   "Who We Are," Competency-Based Education Network, accessed June 21, 2023, www.cbenetwork.org.

welcomed theological educators. These conferences, known as the CBExchange,[3] are powerhouse events, featuring several hundred attendees from across North America and the world. At times, there has been a CBTE track, funded in part by the Association of Theological Schools (ATS), and it has been a fruitful meeting place for theological educators in the development and sharing of expertise with a specific interest to CBTE.

Another source of resources, focused specifically on CBE, is the *Journal of Competency-Based Education*.[4] While the journal is now unfortunately out of print, it is another credible source of academic research about competency-based forms of education, and there is still a rich treasure of back issues available. While much of what was published here is focused on K–12 and college/university models, theological educators can find these materials to be an important source of valid research that can support and substantiate the value of competency-based models to skeptical faculty and board members.

As mentioned before, one of the few book-length treatments of CBE written by Paul LeBlanc, the president of Southern New Hampshire University, is one of the first schools to invent and adopt CBE methodology on a wide scale. His *Students First: Equity, Access, and Opportunity in Higher Education* tells that story and provides a rationale for competency-based programming.[5] LeBlanc was also a keynote speaker at a recent biennial meeting of the ATS.

Seminaries and theological schools will find that groups like the ATS often offer workshops, webinars, podcasts, and learning opportunities focused on CBTE. Along with the ATS, look to the In Trust Center, the Wabash Center for Teaching and Learning, and the Association for Biblical Higher Education (ABHE), all of

---

3   CBExchange, accessed June 21, 2023, https://www.cbexchange.org.
4   *Journal of Competency-Based Education*, Wiley Online Library, accessed June 21, 2023, https://onlinelibrary.wiley.com/journal/23796154.
5   Paul LeBlanc, *Students First: Equity, Access, and Opportunity in Higher Education* (Cambridge, MA: Harvard Education, 2021).

which have offered these sorts of opportunities in recent years.

Symporus is another resource for those looking to develop CBTE programs.[6] Symporus offers a suite of services, technology, and pathways to accreditation for organizations and schools interested in CBTE. Symporus teammates have consulted with dozens of schools and agencies, helping several of them in the areas of program design, curriculum development, stakeholder engagement, program production, and more. By benefiting from these kinds of services, schools can move more quickly to achieve their objectives by taking advantage of established best practices.

While technological resources are discussed elsewhere, one area of resourcing critical to the success of CBTE programs relates to library and journal access. Of course, this challenge will be well known to any school that has offered online programming of any kind. We can, however, offer a couple of resources that theological schools have found helpful in establishing their CBTE programs.

Faithlife has shown itself willing to offer its industry-leading Logos Bible Software program and its thousands of digitized theological books to CBTE schools, often at favorable volume discounts.[7] Some schools have been able to customize libraries specific to the purposes of their program by working with Faithlife.

Another rich resource utilized by CBTE schools is the Digital Theological Library, which offers access to a vast array of digital resources in the theological realm.[8] Through group subscription, schools can allow learners almost any resource currently published in digital form, including journals.

Of course, there are also the more traditional digital sources like ATLA and EBSCO, well known to anyone who has engaged theological education over the last few decades. Also, schools can make their physical libraries available to learners with local

---

6   Symporus, accessed June 21, 2023, www.symporus.com. Full disclosure: Greg and Kent are founding executive partners for Symporus.
7   Faithlife, accessed June 21, 2023, www.faithlife.com.
8   The Digital Theological Library, accessed June 21, 2023, https://libguides.thedtl.org/home.

access.

As the work of competency-based theological education grows, we expect to see the resources develop as well. We are hearing, for example, of groups that are developing mentor certification programs and student support networks for CBTE. As each of us continues in this pioneering work, the resourcing we provide for each other will help to quicken the advance of this movement for the good of all.

FINANCIAL MODELS

"Follow the money" is great advice in investigative journalism. If you want to understand what an organization really values, or how a system truly works, look closely at how the money is managed. We have said repeatedly that competency-based theological education is a set of values more than it is a particular model. If that is true, then those values will be reflected in how the money works.

Christian higher education can be an expensive business. Graduates are not likely to be exceptionally well paid within their careers, meaning that student debt is a nonstarter. A values-based approach to CBTE means that we have to find a way for these programs to be affordable. Learners need a price point that will not require extraordinary cost. We believe that institutions need to find ways to reduce the cost to educate their learners.

There are other values important to a financial model for CBTE. One is that faculty and mentors need to be paid fairly, at least equal to the school's regular compensation structure. This must be achieved without extraordinary fundraising or grant-writing efforts, otherwise the program will not be sustainable and will not be able to scale.

Another area of financial concern is that CBTE programs should aim to be profitable even if the number of learners in the program is relatively small. The value to be served on this point is our sense of missional service. The customized nature of CBTE programming means that sometimes we will want to serve niche, missional interests. We want to be able to do that without requiring large cohorts to carry the program financially.

A further area of monetary consideration relates to the challenge of contextual opportunity. If we value the ability to meet people in their need wherever they are in the world, we will need to attend to the challenge of different currencies, different economic capacities, and differing expectations for price, compensation, and profitability. Sometimes related to culture and sometimes to pure economics, we need to build enough flex into our financial systems so that the financial models do not countermand our educational values.

The arithmetic required to achieve this kind of model might seem almost magical to financial officers who have struggled mightily to keep their schools solvent, but this is one of the benefits of CBTE. We have shown that such a result is possible in our schools and programs. Our schools have done well financially without respect to the size or scale of our programs. We believe that others can see similar results.

In fact, we have to. We can build the most wonderful competency-based educational framework in the world, but if the money doesn't match the model we will fail in delivering on our values. To discern whether an organization means what they say about what they value, again, follow the money.

Just as there is no one correct way of modeling a CBTE program, a school can take a variety of approaches regarding finances. Models will vary for all of the reasons described above. The key is to structure a system that offers the variability necessary to deliver for learners and employers in their contexts.

As a school launches a CBTE program, our recommendation is to create means by which the resources (money, time, etc.) can be tracked separately from the conventional programs in place at the school. This ensures that financial results are not lost in the slush of the larger institutional budget. CBTE programs are apples compared to conventional programs' oranges. If they aren't separated, the risk could compromise competency-based values, due to the subtle pressures of the larger budget. Over time, this can change as needed. At the beginning, however, it can be very helpful to have them tracked separately.

It should be said, at this point, that it might not be wise to expect CBTE programs to save a school, especially if the school is running an array of conventional programs that are losing money and sinking the school. Let those programs show their financial credibility (or not) on their own terms. If, in time, the CBTE programs grow to the extent that they can carry other programming, that is a nice result. But the success of competency-based programs should not depend on their ability to carry programs that have shown their weakness over time.

Another benefit to keeping these two initiatives separate is that conventional programming will not be threatened by this newfangled CBTE stuff. No one's jobs will be at stake if they do not change or adapt to the new (at least until results are proven over time). No program will be endangered by this foray into innovation, as long as the two are separate. From the competency-based side, innovative efforts will likewise not be threatened by the slow, sucking effect of programs that have been sinking over time.

So how does a school build an effective financial model for CBTE? We suggest starting with the tuition rate. If learners cannot afford to study in conventional programs without incurring significant debt, we don't like the chances of success. Start close to home and discern a rate that is affordable for learners without them needing to borrow significantly or take side jobs that will slow them down in their studies and compromise their work.

In our cases, we have found that the sweet spot seems to be around 50 percent of the tuition rate charged by an average school for similar work in your region. Just saying that is an indictment upon the conventional higher education system, which is substantially founded upon the ability of the learner to access student aid. We think that is trouble, in that it makes the school dependent on external players (i.e., governments, regulators, etc.) that direct learning based upon their needs rather than the school's. It's cleaner for everyone if we just charge less. Thus far, it seems that if we can charge no more than half of the average tuition, whether by subscription or by credit hour, our programs will be attractive and our learners will not sink themselves financially.

And yes, we think that schools should consider charging by subscription for educational efforts. Just like Netflix offers all that one can select from their menu of programs, we can do the same with our competency-based programs. In fact, some schools are considering this for their conventional programming as well. This approach to finance offers cost certainty to both learner and school while giving more than lip service to the idea of on-demand education.

Another factor related to tuition rates is the ability to scale to various global (or even domestic) economic variances. For example, we have charged various rates for our programs that are offered in various parts of the world. For example, one such program offered in Colombia was pegged at 50 percent of the tuition "rack rate" (what we would charge in North America). Of course, the mentors, operating in the same economic climate, were compensated at the same proportion. The loser in this sense might be the school, although we have found that many global situations make up in learner volume for any loss in base tuition. In cases where they don't, a decision is made about whether we want to go forward. As described earlier, the key is that we don't lose money. The money coming in must always exceed the money going out.

Speaking of money going out, a further consideration in building a financial model is giving fair consideration to what faculty and mentors will be paid. As stated earlier, we cannot make the case for CBTE on the expectation that faculty will work for less. Not only is it not fair to the labor that makes the program go, but it would be an unnecessary brake on the program's ability to grow. It is far better to pay what the work is worth.

Our approach is to discern what we have to pay our faculty and mentors based roughly on the 50-percent-of-tuition principle, and then scale the expectation for work to a suitable level. We would calculate the number of hours required of mentors and divide the work in ways that fit well within the pay structure. For example, in some of our programs, we employ proctors or program managers, whose job it is to handle some of the work of monitoring, managing, and just generally making sure the trains run on time. Typically, these folks work for the school, handle a larger student load, and are paid less because they are not required to handle everything. Another advantage to the school is that it allows for a smoother functioning program with less dependence upon busy mentors.

The key to all of this is that mentors are paid per capita. This principle takes the risk out of the program for the school, assuring that the money in always exceeds the money out. We have found that there are plenty of qualified mentors available to us anywhere in the world. When learner numbers warrant, we are able to turn faculty mentor positions into full-time faculty jobs, because we have been sure to set our rates accordingly from the beginning. To reiterate, we strive to limit mentor compensation to 50 percent of the tuition that comes in. That leaves 50 percent of the revenue for the school to cover costs, including the base operational structure of the school.

The assumption is that most schools are going to have a base operational structure—president, dean, registrar, and so on. Often, these base operations are funded by multiple revenue streams—endowments, grants, gifts, and tuition. These costs can be alleviated by the profit margin accrued from the school's CBTE programs. The point to realize, however, is that if schools expect CBTE programs to carry these foundational costs, a large number of learners will need to be recruited. Of course, in our opinion, this is also how the viability of conventional programs should be considered.

One other cost that must be considered out of the school's 50 percent is digital library resources. These can be purchased on be-half of the learners, who are scattered around the world but need access to electronic libraries. These costs usually amount to a small portion of the school's cut of tuition. Schools could also leverage the Digital Theological Library.

Of course, the learner will have expenses of his or her own. It is important that they be charged something, however, as this helps them keep skin in the game. Tuition rates can be reduced by scholarships, as can living expenses. However, in our experience, the most significant aspect of this form of cost accrues to the learner's context. If a church or agency is employing the learner, it should be willing to contribute to the learner's living expenses. Sometimes this is done by stipend; sometimes it is done by providing room and board. The point is that the organization is getting value from this proposition and is usually happy to contribute. The rate they will pay is usually lower than a permanent, full-time employee, but the benefit to the organization is substantial.

We have found that these principles and proportions serve well so that we can match money to mission without compromising values. Follow the money to a flourishing competency-based program.

MENTOR DEVELOPMENT

If CBTE is going to work, we are going to need great mentors. The quality of our programs in competency-based theological education rests fully on the character and capacity of those who guide and assess the learners. Perfect systems are no match for poor mentors.

One way to think about CBTE is to imagine it as a system of replication. The model is designed to develop learners in the form of those who mentor them. So, if we want to have proficient graduates, we need to have productive mentors who see the value of reproducing the best of themselves in others who will follow and sustain a sense of mutual mission.

None of this is going to happen by accident. Mentors, like graduates, need to be developed. Early in the formation of a CBTE program, there might be a handful of potential mentors who emerge. The uniqueness of this program often attracts creative, early-adopting mentors who are excited by the potential for something new and promising. But as the program grows, a system of mentor development is required. Developing an effective mentor-training process is one of the ways a CBTE program can be sustained.

The best way to train mentors for competency-based programs is by using competency-based methods. Of course, that will not be so obvious to those of us who default toward seminars, workshops, and courses. It ought to be self-evident that the strongest mentors will be graduates of your program. One of our most delightful experiences is working with second-generation situations, where a graduate offers to mentor someone else. Having been through the program, they understand how to optimize the process for those they lead. This also gives the next-generation learner a sense of confidence that the goal can be reached and that the process is sound.

This is also a fine method of mentor generation. Graduates who have profited from the experience are often hungry to pay it forward. Therefore, the CBTE system becomes self-generating, creating a potentially exponential result for the mission. As each graduate mentors one or more emerging learners, the entire system swells with motivated people.

It is true, nonetheless, that some of the mentors will inevitably lack experience. We have found that it is wise to put these first-experience mentors on teams with experienced mentors. It always goes more smoothly when a new mentor can learn alongside other mentors who have worked within the system previously. This kind of learning-by-doing is faithful to and consistent with the competency-based approach, again allowing the system to self-replicate.

These organic approaches to mentor recruitment are important, though some intentional mentor recruitment might be necessary, particularly with respect to academic or faculty mentors. In our experience there are plenty of people, in most communities, who have the academic background necessary to qualify them to mentor at the appropriate level. Many of these folks will be pleased to collaborate, in part because they are looking for a way to fulfill their sense of gifting for teaching but also because they are intrigued or enthused about the competency-based approach. Others will be motivated by the learner in question, especially if they have a preexisting relationship with the learner.

We have seldom found it difficult to find the vocational mentors, or those who will serve the learner in context. It is rare, in our experience, to find a learner who qualifies for this kind of program who does not have an experienced and qualified mentor in the field that they can look to. Most vocational mentors come with an innate understanding that mentoring the next generation of leaders is part of their calling. The only challenge with folks like these is making sure that they appreciate and understand the specific form of mentoring that they are called to offer.

We have said that our preferred form of mentor training is organic, using the same contextual development approach that we use with the learners themselves. However, that doesn't mean that we should not put together some kind of formalized, front-end means of making mentors aware of the expectations to which they will be accountable.

Typically, this kind of training is done through personal one-on-one instruction and guidance when the program is smaller or just getting started. As the program grows and the school gains experience, more sophisticated training can be developed. Schools would be wise to offer this kind of mentor training on the same online platform that they will be using with their learners. Whether using the Pathwright platform that we recommend below or some other tool, getting mentors trained on the same system that they will use with their learners gives them an advantage as they grow to understand what will be expected of them. In our experience, mentor training is best facilitated by others who are engaged in the work of mentoring learners. Often, the training process will include content that describes the educational philosophy, an opportunity to reflect on that content, and then a series of experiences focused on helping new mentors engage in an action-reflection process wherein they work with a learner under the guidance and support of another more experienced mentor. The driving force behind all of the training is a set of outcomes and indicators that describe effective mentors.

The biggest concern is whether mentors can embrace and embody the values of the school's program and of CBTE in general as well as deepen their understanding of topics like collaborative mission, contextual discipleship, integration of outcomes, customized proficiency, value of teamwork, and holistic assessment.

One of the more surprising aspects of mentor training for CBTE is the challenge of untraining them from the assumptions and presuppositions that they will be bringing with them into the process. Our experience is that even people who come from outside the world of academics have a deeply ingrained sense of what education or curriculum is supposed to look like. It will take some time and effort to break mentors free from the strongholds of the semester system and the credit-hour currency. Many mentors will be attracted to this brave new world of academic assessment, but they will still struggle not to default back to old ways of operating.

One of those strongholds is the influence of time on the educational process. It takes some persistence to help mentors appreciate that some learners will be able to satisfy some outcomes quickly due to previous, proven competency, while others are going to have to take longer durations of time to show sustained and not temporary proficiency.

The integrative approach is another tough mental nut for mentors to crack. The academic enterprise has been siloed for so long that it is hard for mentors to consider how to effectively combine biblical study, theological understanding, practical capacity, and character development. The best-trained mentors will understand the system and will be able to look for proficiency across all aspects of the outcome.

Speaking with one voice is an essential aspect of the mentor team experience, regardless of the various roles played by members of the mentor team. This will require mentors to learn to be in conversation with each other about their assessment of the learner.

The best mentors will know the program and system so well that they will be able to take advantage of all of the options to the benefit of the learner and ministry context. Mentors need to know the specifics of the program they are serving as it relates to things like dealing with learner failure, the grading approach, assignment customization, and recognition of prior learning and proficiency. They are not going to get all of that right from the start but, as they participate in the mentoring process alongside proven and experienced mentors, they will learn to work the system to the benefit of the learner and their context, like a well-trained musician.

One of the main interests that we need to build into mentors is to help them appreciate the importance of timely portfolio input. Learners prove their development of proficiency through the submission of their materials into their online portfolio. Good mentoring involves timely responses so that the learner is not left hanging, wondering whether the work they have submitted is thoughtful and acceptable. Mentoring needs to be in the moment, taking advantage of learning experiences as they happen. Good mentors will keep up with their learners, informing them if there is a reason they have to step back for a period of time (vacations, for example).

In the end, mentoring is about the relationship between the learner and the guide. When building CBTE programs, it is important to put sufficient effort into preparing those who will oversee learners.

Mentoring can become an intimate relationship. It is difficult to train someone toward trustworthiness and the willingness to be vulnerable. But the same qualities we want to see in our mentors are the qualities we want to develop in our learners. The best way to get there is through time and intention—the essence of mentoring.

LEVERAGING TECHNOLOGY

In our section on flexible technology, we noted that CBTE requires a shift in technology that supports the paradigm shift in educational philosophy. In particular, we invited schools to consider choosing their technology based on whether it (1) encourages customization and consistency, (2) uses a mobile-first stack of solutions, (3) puts humans first, and (4) allows for flexible pricing. In this section, we are facing design strategies, which means that we are going to suggest a few practical implications of the commitments listed earlier in the book. Along the way, we will make a few observations, offer a few recommendations, and extend an invitation.

A Few Observations

When leveraging technology within CBTE, we have learned that it is important to pay attention to three aspects of the educational philosophy: mentor engagement, customized pathways, and distributed and multimodal learning. When considering which software solution your school might use for its CBTE program, we think these three considerations are of the utmost importance.

Often, schools run CBTE programs by leveraging the software they are currently using for their traditional programs. We understand the attractive nature of this approach and are fully aware that, in some cases, the school is already financially committed to a particular type of software. That being said, if it is possible to consider new software for a CBTE program, we encourage every school to do so. In most cases, the legacy software that our schools have been using will not adequately serve learners, mentors, and educational partners. Obviously, work-arounds are possible. However, in our experience, they often create more work and cost than using a software that better serves CBTE (and, therefore, learners, mentors, partners, etc.). Here are a few reasons why.

Mentor engagement. One of the things that sets CBTE apart from the wider world of CBE (and conventional education) is the way in which mentors are engaged in the process. Most schools use multiple mentors, and we have suggested that mentor teams are a vital aspect of formative, high-quality CBTE. Prior to writing this book, we studied a wide array of learning management systems in search of something that could serve us well. In that search, we found that most technology solutions simply don't have an effective way to work with mentor teams. Those that do often fail to have adequate features for developing learning pathways.

When exploring technology solutions, it is important to pay

close attention to how mentors can and will be engaged. Ideally, mentors can follow learners through the entire process without the school having to enroll mentors in the same learning experiences. For example, most learning management systems are structured around courses, which means that connections between people are driven by courses. In that kind of structure, schools often need to build a different section of every course in order to have a discussion group that includes only the learner and her mentors—a very time-intensive and therefore expensive endeavor. A better technological solution will use people as the organizing principle, which means mentors can be connected to their learners regardless of what they are learning. In this approach, the mentor team only sees what the learner is doing even if the learner is in a course with several other learners. In addition, the technology needs to be highly intuitive so that the school's IT support team is not overwhelmed by an influx of questions from the distributed mentor team.

Customized pathways. As noted earlier, customized proficiency is a key principle of CBTE. Technology solutions will have a deep impact on the level to which a school's institution can follow this principle. It is common for learning management and learner information systems to be designed around the assumption that each learner is going to take the exact same path through a degree. CBTE, on the other hand, invites us to recognize that learning is nonlinear. The implication, therefore, is that we need technology solutions that allow mentor teams to customize the learning pathway for each learner. In practice, this can take many forms. The key is making sure the institution keeps that in mind when looking at technology solutions. A simple question to ask is, If two learners were in the same program, how would the software allow mentor teams to adjust the course/competency/learning pathway in light of each learner's needs?

Distributed and multimodal learning. Finally, each CBTE program that we have worked with thus far has a distributed student body (i.e., not in the same geographic location) that engages in multiple types of learning modalities (e.g., in-person, online, asynchronous, synchronous, experiential, project-based). The learning management systems need to account for that kind of diversity. It must allow mentor teams, learners, and faculty to work with each other across location and time while accounting for everything from scheduled or predefined learning to self-paced and/or asynchronous learning of all types.

A Few Recommendations

Given those observations, we have a few recommendations. You might be able to call these "lessons from the front lines." That is to say, we have worked in the field for a number of years and have been in conversations with schools, accreditors, software companies, federal and provincial regulators in the United States and Canada, an array of denominations, nonprofit organizations, and much more. In that time, we have come across a few tools that seem to work well—which, at the time of writing, are the following.

Pathwright. Our go-to recommendation for learning management software is Pathwright. It is a next-generation platform that takes a human-centered approach to software development and learning design.[9]

Airtable. If you are looking for a database solution as flexible as the information you need to store in it, Airtable is a good choice. We are convinced that schools could build their entire student information system in Airtable. The key here is finding a system that doesn't lock the institution into a data structure that assumes traditional learning.[10]

Zapier. Customized learning doesn't mean "manual" or "labo-

---

9   Pathwright, accessed June 21, 2023, www.pathwright.com.
10   Airtable, accessed June 21, 2023, www.airtable.com.

rious" processes. Zapier is a great tool for automating workflows. It allows the school to connect various pieces of software without needing to know how to write code. For example, registration and payment processes can be created that account for distributed and multimodal learning through automations that connect Pathwright, Airtable, and Stripe.[11]

Stripe. You may already use this one and simply not know it. Stripe is a payment processing system used by organizations all over the world. Its APIs (see below) are robust, and it works with more than 135 currencies.[12]

REST APIs. This recommendation and the next one are not specific software solutions (i.e., applications or platforms), but rather things to keep in mind. An API (application programming interface) is a set of definitions and protocols that aid in the building and integration of applications. It's a way for different pieces of software to communicate with each other. In our experience over the past fifteen years or so, applications that leverage REST APIs tend to be a better fit with distributed and multimodal learning. This is usually because they are generally considered easier to use and tend to be faster and more lightweight than other types of APIs (which means that they can often scale more easily, too). Obviously, these are our opinions and others are welcome to disagree; we are simply sharing our experience—and our recommendation. When looking at software solutions, we encourage consideration of applications that leverage REST APIs.

Symporus. Finally, we encourage schools to consult with Symporus along the way. In full disclosure, we helped found Symporus

---

11 At the time of writing, Zapier works with more than five thousand apps and can be found at www.zapier.com (accessed June 21, 2023).

12 At the time of writing, more than 90 percent of adults in the United States have purchased something from a business that uses Stripe. It can be found at http://www.stripe.com (accessed June 21, 2023).

and continue to be involved in its work. Symporus was founded as a collaboration between Pathwright, Northwest Seminary and College, and Kairos University for the purpose of empowering fresh expressions of theological education. It provides services, software, and pathways to accreditation for organizations who want to build, operate, or enhance CBTE programs. It has a wide array of experience in multiple countries, at multiple educational levels, and in various forms. It helped Pathwright envision and test the mentor engagement features that are now part of that software platform, and it has helped numerous organizations build and customize software solutions that fit the needs of CBTE.[13]

An Invitation

Our invitation is short and sweet: we invite schools to leverage technology in ways that support customized learning. The gravitational pull toward using software that already exists within our institutions is quite strong. CBTE presents an opportunity to try something new. Seize that opportunity and consider new approaches. On the front end, it may seem like extra work and expense. When the dust settles, schools will be happy that they didn't let the software design the learning. Rather, schools will design the learning and then discover technology that can be an accelerant instead of a hindrance.

---

13 Symporus, accessed June 21, 2023, www.symporus.com.

CHAPTER 5

THE PARADIGM SHIFT TOWARD COMPETENCY-BASED THEOLOGICAL EDUCATION

Moving toward a competency-based system requires a different way of thinking about the task of theological education. It is a paradigm shift—a fundamental change in the underlying assumptions around which we do our work.

In science, a shift in paradigm is required when the prevailing norms under which scientists operate prove to be incompatible with emerging new phenomena.[1] We believe that these are the

---

1   Thomas Kuhn, *The Structure of Scientific Revolutions: A Brilliant, Original Analysis of the Nature, Causes, and Consequences of Revolutions in Basic Scientific Concepts* (Chicago: University of Chicago Press, 1962).

conditions facing theological educators today. Our long and closely held behaviors are proving insufficient to the challenges posed by new technologies, skeptical markets, and deep uncertainties in a post-pandemic world. CBTE shows promise as a productive way forward in such times, but we will not get there if we insist on conventional operations. We have to learn to think in reverse.

Conventional forms of education are focused on classrooms and credit hours. The currency of the credit hour is a way of quantifying the presumed value conferred by occupying "seat time" in the classroom.[2] More recent market pressures and technological advances have encouraged schools to move the classroom onto the computer, making use of online learning management systems to extend and make accessible the effects and intentions of the classroom. The hope is that this will have some positive effect on the intended context at some imagined future point. But the paradigm is still centered upon classroom instruction. The assumption is that helping learners toward proficiency of the relevant information will result in a corresponding proficiency of the contextual expectations. This faith may not be entirely sound.

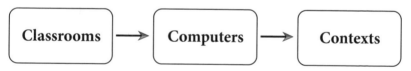

Competency-based approaches reverse the field. CBTE focuses on the interests and opportunities provided by the context, utilizing computers and online resources as supportive mechanisms, introducing classrooms when helpful. It is a reverse-engineered approach to theological education.

---

2   Laitinen, "Cracking the Credit Hour."

Let's not forget that classrooms are great for delivering content. There is an efficiency to the classroom if our intention is to inform student learners. That this is part of the educational task cannot be denied. Yet, this is the easy part of what we do, and it is the place at which we are most vulnerable to other providers that provide content cheaper, faster, glitzier, and by a more prestigious educator than most could afford to employ. This does not have to threaten us if we can appreciate our task as something greater than offering content.

Excellent educators have always understood that they are curators of content, mentoring learners toward proficiency, not only of the information itself but of the competencies and capacities made possible by the information. This is the kind of educational process that CBTE values.

Many educators, attracted to the values of CBTE, will want to dip their toe in the water, cautiously approaching the possibilities offered by this new way of conceiving our task. But it is hard to shift a paradigm without complete commitment. Hybrid approaches are always possible if we are willing to think creatively, but we have to appreciate that compromising the values will result in a compromised result.

Take, for example, the idea of customized proficiency. Proficiency is a worthy objective, much valued by the agencies we serve, but proficiency takes time—probably more time than our conventional three-and-a-half-month semesters will allow. It might take more than a semester for even the best learners to prove proficiency of a critical aspect of character development or theological transformation. We can certainly frame our conventional courses more faithfully around outcomes; that would be the least we could do. Yet, we should not hold the illusion that even reasonable proficiency will be possible for every learner within arbitrary timelines, which are governed more by our institutional interests than by the interests of the church or missional agency that we hope to walk alongside. Hybrid approaches, in our experience, will produce less than half the result of a fully realized CBTE program.

That said, we recognize that a wholesale change to an institutional culture may be daunting, and, perhaps, even unwise. We do not have to throw out everything that we have built over many decades to try something new and uncertain. Our recommendation is that we start by building something to the side of our conventional programs. Think of this, at least initially, as a kind of "skunkworks" project that can be fed and watered until the degree to which it can empower your objectives becomes clear.[3] Identify a group of early adopters who willingly embrace the promise of this concept. As the project gains strength, buy-in will grow from those served but also from those providing the service. With good work, the results will become evident, and the wins will accumulate. Others will want to join the initiative. Eventually constituencies will begin to demand it. Schools might never completely abandon conventional programs. We haven't. But the things that will be learned through this project will enhance even the older programs as the values become ubiquitous within the organizational culture.

The key is to make sure that the institutional system allows for the shift that CBTE requires. Schools would do well to take a hard look at every academic, enrollment, and learner service function. Sometimes the processes with which we are most familiar can present unconscious barriers to the work that we intend. We are going to have to be persistent in our pursuit of our values, and we are going to have to be loving toward those who will be slower to adopt. It took us a thousand years to develop our current patterns of education. It might take us a little while to reinvent ourselves.

In the meantime, we can give each other room. We do not have to force the hand of the unwilling. They will come around as they see that the results are in keeping with their own sense of calling. We can be patient in keeping with the advice we learned from Richard

---

3   "Skunkworks" is a commonplace business term, originally developed by the Lockheed Martin aerospace company. The term describes an innovative undertaking involving a limited number of hand-selected people outside the normal research and development structure of the company. See https://www.lockheedmartin.com/en-us/who-we-are/business-areas/aeronautics/skunkworks.html.

Mouw, the former president of Fuller Theological Seminary. Rich was quoting a friend of his about how to reach out to colleagues who are not yet on board with CBTE: "Don't argue back with them. Give them some room to save face."[4] Keep in mind how much we are asking of people. We are encouraging individuals to rethink fundamental aspects of their calling and their livelihoods. It will be easier for people to eventually come back around to a new way of being if we have been gracious from the start.

Change is never an easy proposition. Humans are creatures of habit, subject to a natural inertia. Inertia, unlike inertness, describes our tendency to continue in an existing state of rest or uniform motion until such time as an external force demands a change. We are in motion, but it is a comfortable motion. It is an easy way of being, as it requires no new learning and no challenge to our assumptions. It is ironic that educators, of all people, would be content to remain in such a state, given our fundamental interest in growth and understanding. It is doubly troubling that *theological* educators would fall into this trap. Change-resisters were usually the villains of the Bible.

We pursue change, not because there is anything inherently important about shifting paradigms but because we are in a restless state of hunger for God's kingdom. We aspire to something better— something kingdom-shaped—and until we get there, we are willing to examine any change that might be productive in pursuit of the things to which God has called us. God is in motion. His kingdom is "at hand" (to quote Jesus), which means that stasis is not an option.

Competency-based theological education is more than just another model. It is certainly suited for the challenges of a post-pandemic world. If we have learned anything, it is that our offerings must be closer to the ground where people live and move. We have been delighted, for example, to observe how CBTE learners have

---

4   Richard J. Mouw, "Broadening the Evangelical Vision: 'Needs' and 'Wants' in Theo-
     logical Education," in *Disruption and Hope: Religious Traditions and the Future of
     Theological Education*, ed. Barbara G. Wheeler (Waco, TX: Baylor University Press,
     2019), 91.

been able to thrive in their work, even in periods of virus-required isolation.

CBTE is more than just financially efficient. We celebrate anything that can make theological education more affordable to learners and more viable for schools. CBTE has that in its favor, but that in itself would not be enough for us.

CBTE offers a better way for us to pursue our mission. It results in learners who have developed and displayed actual proficiency of the knowledge, skills, and character traits that are necessary to their calling and to the mission of those groups that they will serve. They come from the process tested and proven, trustworthy servants who will make it for the long haul. Our experience is that CBTE produces the best possible graduates at the best possible price. It is the most missional thing that we could be doing, which is why we have been willing to share this with you in these pages. It will take courage and it will require conviction, but these are things that we can find as God leads us and empowers us by the Spirit.

We are calling you to consider a back-to-the-future kind of opportunity. When we stood ready to launch our first programs, we went to our community for a final sense of confirmation. We were about to take a giant leap into an uncertain future, and we wanted someone to affirm that we were not crazy.

One of our mentors, Larry Perkins, was especially affirming. "I liken this to the ancient models of education," he said, referring to classic mentoring models developed a thousand years ago at places like Oxford and Cambridge. Perhaps we are not reinventing the wheel, but rediscovering it.

"Mentored proficiency in context" is the way that Jesus trained his own disciples, and one could not want any better than that. Jesus walked with those he trained. There were moments of instruction that one could almost imagine happening in a classroom (were such a thing available), but those things were deepened and affirmed through long conversations over significant periods of time as the context offered opportunities to apply instruction in real time. Jesus was a competency-based theological educator before it was ever a trend.

We might be shifting the current paradigm. But perhaps we are just shifting it back to its original, intended place, in our own way and time. It will require conviction, but it will result in good things for our learners and for those ministries they serve. We will gain the courage to match our educational paradigm to the trajectory of the kingdom, and we will see that kingdom come on earth as it is in heaven.

APPENDIX

QUALITY FRAMEWORK FOR COMPETENCY-BASED THEOLOGICAL EDUCATION

The following is proposed as a framework for competency-based theological education in keeping with the principles and practices of this book. It is derived from a variety of similar documents developed by the Competency-Based Education Network and some of the early adopting CBTE schools. Working within this framework can help ensure quality in curriculum development and program delivery.

EDUCATIONAL VALUES

Programs and curriculum developed and delivered through CBTE will be guided by the following educational values.

Collaborative Mission
    CBTE programs and curriculum will be designed in collaboration with voices outside of the institution, particularly those from organizations, employers, networks, or communities in which learners reside. Such curriculum must be designed in dialogue with these voices, to ensure alignment and cultural fit.

Contextual Discipleship
    CBTE curriculum will be offered in context, understanding that the most profound and resilient learning develops from relevant praxis. Framing learning as discipleship in context appreciates that a learner's growth in Christ will be evident in one's relationships and experiences.

Integrated Outcomes
    CBTE curriculum will detail the outcomes that describe a formed graduate who can be trusted to embody the traits and capacities required for the expected purpose. These outcomes must recognize the integrated nature of knowledge—content, character, and craft—by attending to all three dimensions and to one's theological commitments.

Customized Proficiency
    CBTE programs are focused on demonstrating proficiency within contextually conceived outcomes, without concern for time. Such outcomes are customized to the unique requirements of the learner and situation and reflect the standards of excellence relevant to that particular community. These programs focus on the learner's proof of proficiency, however that is developed and displayed, without undue regard for the systems and structures that may be helpful in getting the learner to that point.

Team-Based Mentoring
    CBTE curriculum depends upon teams of academic and contextual mentors committed to each learner, who can observe and

assess the learner's development and display of proficiency over time. These mentors walk together with the learner, speaking with one voice in the nurture, critique, and encouragement of the learner in their charge.

Holistic Assessment

CBTE programs act as a system of assessment, focused on the learner's observed proficiency across all aspects of the described outcomes. These programs attend to ongoing assessment of all aspects of the work, including mentor commitment and overall program effectiveness.

OUTCOME CONSTRUCTION

Outcomes are focused on discrete learning expectations, describing an integration of the content, character, and craft necessary for proficiency. These outcomes are constructed to allow the learner opportunity to both develop and display proficiency in live context to the satisfaction of their mentors. Outcomes comprise the following four elements:

Articulation

The outcome must be expressed in clear but comprehensive and measurable language *so that* all stakeholders have an effective grasp on the description of proficiency.

Indicators

The outcome should be restated in terms of an itemized list of observable and measurable behaviors, skills, attitudes, dispositions, and/or cognitive abilities to be demonstrated by the learner. These indicators are written so that the learner and mentors know what to look for and can recognize proficiency when it has been achieved.

Inputs

Each outcome offers a list of inputs that could be helpful to the learner in his or her development and display of proficiency. Such inputs could include conventional forms like lectures and prescribed reading; or they might be more creative, including such means as podcasts, seminars, structured conversations, and experiences. These inputs must be accessible to the learner during the period of study. In addition to those provided by the institution, mentors and learners should feel free to suggest additional or alternative pieces that might be of greater use to a particular learner in his or her context. For that reason, inputs should only be listed as compulsory when strictly necessary to an organizational partner or employment objective.

Interactions

Each outcome offers a list of interactions that could be helpful to the learner in his or her development and display of proficiency. Such interactions would include any activity, project, or engagement that could advance the learner's capacity to display the stated outcome. These could include conventional forms like writing papers or taking exams, but they could also include more creative means such as interviews, service projects, video production, situational learning activities, or anything conceivable that could advance the interest of the learner and the program outcomes. Mentors and learners should feel free to suggest additional or alternative interactions that might be of greater use to a particular learner in his or her context. Interactions should only be listed as compulsory when strictly necessary to an organizational partner or employment objective.

SYSTEMS CONSIDERATIONS

CBTE programs will work toward a number of systemic considerations, including the following.

Learners and Contexts

Learners should be enrolled in a CBTE program only when there is suitable vocational context available with the agreement of a group of mentors who are committed to observe and assess the learner on the ground. Significant front-end discernment is recommended.

Time Frame for Completion

CBTE programs operate outside conventional academic systems like semesters. Time is not a primary factor in the learner's pursuit of proficiency, except where excessive delay and delinquency display the learner's incapacity to complete the work within a reasonable expectation.

Platform

Learners and mentors must display evidence of the student's learning and the mentors' encouragement on a platform that serves as a digital record of learning.

OUTCOME EXAMPLE

The following, developed by Kent Anderson, is suggested as an example of an outcome description suitable for a CBTE program. Notice that the inputs and interactions are offered as a kind of menu of options for the learners and mentors in pursuit of the larger outcome. We offer it so that you can see the kinds of things that are possible in outcome design. Of course, your creativity could take it much further.

Outcome Articulation: Effective Communication

The learner will develop the capacity to communicate effectively both verbally and nonverbally, publicly and privately, formally and informally, and in written and oral forms. The learner will display the capacity to rally their team around a shared vision, inspiring people through the building of trust and morale in changing and diverse environments. Followers will know they can trust what the learner says as they speak with clarity, integrity, and conviction. The learner will display skill in advancing the interests of the organization in their communication of goals and strategies, speaking in ways that minimize misunderstanding and ambiguity.

Indicators

- The learner communicates effectively in all contexts necessary to their leadership
- The learner inspires people toward a shared vision within changing and diverse environments.
- Followers know that the learner can be trusted because they speak with clarity, integrity, and conviction.
- The learner advances the interests of their organization by the way they communicate.
- The learner speaks in ways that minimize misunderstanding and ambiguity.

Inputs

Anderson, Kenton C. *Integrative Preaching: A Comprehensive Model for Transformational Proclamation.* Grand Rapids: Baker, 2017.

Blaisdell, Bob. *Great Speeches of the 20th Century.* New York: Dover, 2011.

Cialdini, Robert B. *Influence: The Psychology of Persuasion.* San Francisco: Harper Business, 2006.

Dudeck, Joe. "2022 Trends and Best Practices—Social Media." Keyhole Marketing, January 30, 2022. https://www.keyhole-marketing.us/social-media-best-practices.

Hipps, Shane. *Flickering Pixels: How Technology Shapes Your Faith.* Grand Rapids: Zondervan, 2009.

Koessler, John. *Folly, Grace, and Power: The Mysterious Act of Preaching.* Grand Rapids: Zondervan, 2011.

McClellan, Dave. *Preaching by Ear: Speaking God's Truth from the Inside Out.* Wooster, OH: Weaver, 2014.

McLuhan, Marshall. *Understanding Media: The Extensions of Man.* New York: McGraw-Hill, 1964.

Morand, Tatiana. "The Ultimate Social Media Guide for Nonprofits." Personify—Wild Apricot. https://www.wildapricot.com/blog/social-media-guide-for-nonprofits.

Ong, Walter. *Orality and Literacy: The Technologizing of the Word.* London: Methuen, 1982.

Postman, Neil. *Amusing Ourselves to Death: Public Discourse in the Age of Show Business.* New York: Viking, 1985.

Schultz, Quentin. *An Essential Guide to Public Speaking: Serving Your Audience with Faith, Skill, and Virtue.* Grand Rapids: Baker Academic, 2006.

Seminar on Effective Communication, Providence University College, Otterburne, MB, to be offered occasionally online or in person.

Interactions

Principles of public speaking. Building directly and demonstrably from the Schultz reading, the learner will describe a set of five to ten principles of public speaking that she or he intends will govern the practice of his or her public speaking. These principles will be described and presented to the mentors in a brief paper of three to five pages. The learner will include various examples of his or her personal use of these principles.

Formal communication. The learner will display their capacity for formal, large-group communication by presenting a series of at least three lectures, sermons, or public addresses to an audience of at least twenty people. The effectiveness of these presentations will be attested by at least five listeners who describe their response in writing, utilizing forms designed for the purpose. The learner will submit to his or her mentors a set of comprehensive developmental notes for these presentations that will show the learner's preparation process for this sort of speaking. The mentors will have personally listened to at least one of these presentations either in person or by video recording.

Persuasion audit. The learner will identify some significant leadership issue requiring persuasive communication to effect a desired transformation. The learner will produce a *persuasion audit* identifying achievable means of influencing the situation around Robert Cialdini's six persuasive elements and describing the result to his or her mentors in a paper of five to eight pages.

Orality and literacy. Building from the Ong and McClellan readings, the learner will form a personal theory of communication, with particular emphasis on the way that orality shapes communication in contemporary culture. The learner will communicate this in either a paper or a visual presentation and share it with a group of other learners or mentees, sharing with the mentor team what the student has learned.

Interpersonal/office communication. The learner will have a thorough conversation with his or her mentors relating to the practice of interpersonal/office communications, showing non-confidential examples of emails, memos, and other forms of communication for input and discussion. The learner will follow up with a set of written principles intended to guide the learner's practice of such communications.

Project proposal. The learner will write a proposal for some significant project (imagined or actual) intended to persuade or convince a board or governing body to adopt or approve its intentions. This proposal will include both a written document and a visual presentation (Keynote, PowerPoint, or something similar). The learner will present the proposal either to a real such body or to his or her mentors, who will role-play the situation. If the learner presents the proposal in real time to an actual governing body, an oral report of the results should be offered to the mentors.

Preaching for transformational effect. Building from the Koessler and Anderson books, the learner will write a five-to-eight-page paper expressing his or her view of preaching and its practice upon the transformation of listeners in the twenty-first century. As part of this project, the learner will describe his or her own approach to the task of preaching, giving examples.

Conversational communication. The learner will pay attention to his or her conversational communications, intending to notice and appreciate patterns and tendencies, both positive and negative. The learner will engage in a feedback session with three people who offer their observations about the learner's conversational practice. This feedback will come from people with whom the learner interacts with on a regular basis. Particular focus will be given to things like the learner's availability, listening skills, clarity of intent, use of humor, show of respect, persuasive capacity, and general amiability. The learner will summarize his or her findings in a two-to-three-page self-evaluation for oral discussion with the mentors.

Small group communication and leadership. The learner will take leadership of a small study group or community (fifteen people or less) for a period of at least three months of weekly or biweekly gatherings. The learner will look to his or her mentors for guidance as to how to gain this opportunity and how to prepare for it. The learner will bring his or her preparation notes to the mentors for feedback before the live presentation. At the end of the period, the learner will gather four or five of those who regularly attended these meetings to provide feedback as to the learner's communication and leadership skills. The learner will then bring that feedback to a conversation with the mentors.

Great speeches. The learner will study and compare two "great speeches" from history, and in a brief document describe the comparative strengths and weaknesses of those speakers while identifying principles that could be helpful in his or her own public speaking.

Social media. The learner will engage in a disciplined use of social media on at least three platforms for a period of three to four months, giving the mentors access to these feeds. Upon completion of that period—and building from the Hipps, Dudeck, and Morand inputs—the learner will describe his or her preferred practice of social media usage in a thorough conversation with the mentors. The learner will also identify four or five well-known and effective users of these platforms, describing what makes these people so beneficial in their use of these platforms.

Technology and infotainment. Building from the McLuhan, Postman, and Hipps readings, the learner will write an eight-to-twelve-page academic paper addressing the question of how modern technology is affecting contemporary society and its communications, for good or for ill.